P9-CAF-079

Résumés
and
Personal
Statements
for
Health
Professionals

James W. Tysinger, PH.D.

GALEN PRESS, LTD.

Copyright © 1994 by Galen Press, Ltd. All rights reserved.

Original cover and inside illustrations by Cathy McLeod for Galen Press, Ltd.
Copyright © 1994 by Galen Press, Ltd. All rights reserved.

No part of this book may be reproduced or transmitted in any form or by any means, electronic or mechanical, including photocopying, recording, or by any information storage and retrieval system, without permission in writing from the Publisher.

Galen Press Ltd.
P.O. Box 64400
Tucson, AZ 85728-4400
602-577-8363
602-529-6459

ISBN: 1-883620-19-8

Library of Congress Cataloging-in-Publication Data

Tysinger , James W. , 1949-
        Résumés and personal statements for health professionals / James
W. Tysinger.
        p.   cm.
        Includes bibliographical references and index.
        ISBN 1-883620-19-8
        1. Résumés (Employment)   2. Medical Personnel--Vocational
guidance.   I. Title.
        R690.T96   1994
        650.14 ' 02461--dc20   94-30274

Velcro is a registered trademark of Velcro USA, Inc.
Microsoft, Word 6, and Windows are registered trademarks of Microsoft Corporation.
Macintosh is a registered trademark of Apple Computer, Inc.
Hewlett-Packard and LaserJet are registered trademarks of Hewlett-Packard Company.
dBase is a registered trademark of Borland International, Inc.
Arial and Times New Roman are registered trademarks of The Monotype Corporation, PLC.
WordPerfect is a registered trademark of WordPerfect Corporation.
Cabbage Patch is a registered trademark of Hasbro, Inc.
Pillsbury is a registered trademark of Pillsbury Company, Inc.

Cover Design by Lynn Bishop Graphics, Tucson, AZ.

10   9   8   7   6   5   4   3   2   1

Printed in the United States of America

CONTENTS

ACKNOWLEDGMENTS

This book was made possible by the assistance and support I received from many others.

First, I gratefully acknowledge the patience and support I received from my wife, Sylvia, and my children: Alan, Sarah, and Amy. Second, I deeply appreciate the encouragement, guidance, and assistance that Mary Lou Iserson, C.P.A. and Kenneth V. Iserson, M.D., M.B.A. supplied in abundant amounts. Third, contributions by Margaret "Peggy" Robbins, a highly skilled graphic artist; Beverly McCabe, Ph.D., R.D.; Donald Witzke, Ph.D.; and Frank Hale, Ph.D. enabled the book to progress smoothly. Fourth, I must acknowledge the assistance of the University of Arizona medical reference librarians, Hannah Fisher, R.N., M.L.S.; Nga T. Nguyen; and Marilyn Hope-Balcerzak; as well as Robert Fisher, M.L.S., reference librarian-at-large. These individuals recognized the need for this book and cheerfully reviewed it during its preparation.

Thanks also to the many students and health professionals who helped me develop résumé and personal statement writing skills. They fueled my interest in the topics and helped me see how appropriate analysis and feedback could improve the communication of one's thoughts. I especially appreciate those individuals who permitted me to modify their résumés and personal statements for this book. A part of these students will always be with me. Reading their works, remembering our toils, and recalling their joys after "matching" or accepting positions always makes me smile.

Finally, thanks to the wonderful professionals at Galen Press, Ltd., who believed in this book's importance, and without whom this book would not have been possible. These include the labor and professional skills supplied by Patti Cassidy and Mary Lou Sherk, whose editing, formatting, and suggestions significantly improved the book's content and readability, and by Cathy McLeod, whose illustrations translated my thoughts into visual images.

PREFACE

Since you are reading this book, you are interested in writing either a résumé (also known as a "curriculum vitae" or a "CV") or a personal statement. You are not alone. Nearly all health professionals need current résumés to apply for their "dream" position. Beginning with admission to school, and continuing into the job market, competition for positions can be fierce. You have to look your best "on paper" so you can obtain an interview.

I've heard "Can you help me with my résumé and personal statement?" many times from desperate people who need these documents. My experience as a teacher and advisor in health education programs for over twenty years, nine of them in medical schools, has taught me how to help. These health professionals faced the same challenges you face when you sit down to write your résumé and personal statement. The strategies that aided them will also help you. Those strategies are contained in this book

My experiences have taught me that people sell themselves short in these documents. Most fail to get their rich and varied backgrounds down on paper. They need guidance and feedback. Some have resources, like me or another advisor, to help them. Many others, though, don't have any resources available when they need them.

This book is designed to fill that void. It will help you prepare a well-written résumé and personal statement that will describe your strengths and accomplishments to employers and selection committees. Your documents cannot make you appear better than you are, but they should help others get to know you before they meet you in person.

I've used real-life illustrations to help you relate to the challenges other people faced when writing their documents. Read these illustrations to avoid common mistakes. I've also included examples of actual résumés and personal statements to enable you to see how others wrote materials that truly depicted their experiences and marketable attributes.

Potential employers and selection committees have a wealth of information in your application packet, but *your personal statement and résumé are the only parts you control.* (You did have indirect input into the transcripts, dean's letter, etc., but you can't do much to influence them now.)

Remember that starting to write is the most difficult part of the process. So, don't just read this book and procrastinate. Begin to write now!

James W. Tysinger, Ph.D.

FEEDBACK FORM

Please return to: James W. Tysinger, Ph.D.
Office of Medical Education, MC9065
University of Texas Southwestern Medical Center at Dallas
5323 Harry Hines Blvd.
Dallas, Texas 75235-9065 USA

If you have an unusual or intriguing résumé or personal statement, and would allow me to use it in the next edition of this book (after changing identifying information), please send it to me at the address above. Include a statement giving me permission to modify and use your document(s). Also include your address and phone number. Also, if you have any suggestions of information or a personal experience to include in the next edition please send them to me.

Include the following in the next edition of this book:

_____

_____

_____

_____

_____

_____

_____

_____

_____

_____

(If you need more space, continue on the back or use another sheet.)

(Optional)   Name: _____

              Address: _____

                       _____

              Phone Number:_____

Thanks for your feedback.

1: Résumés and Personal Statements for Health Professionals: An Overview

Build your résumé using your traits and skills.

How will this book help you?

It will begin by

- answering your questions about résumés.
- helping you develop a "can-do" attitude about writing a résumé.
- giving you a method for identifying your personal accomplishments.

1

- showing you how to describe your accomplishments to emphasize your strengths.

- leading you through a writing process that will help you produce a polished and marketable résumé.

- supplying you with multiple examples of excellent résumés for health professionals.

Then, it will

- show you how to design a personal statement.

- provide you with examples of personal statements that worked for their authors.

- lead you through the process of writing a personal statement.

And finally, it will

- describe the best ways to use your résumé and personal statement.

- provide incentives to continue refining and adding to your skills.

- explain the use of cover letters to establish relationships with reviewers.

- show the importance of using thank-you letters following interviews.

- give examples of thank-you and cover letters.

The job or school application material that you submit is a reflection of you. Because it will be used as a deciding factor in granting you an all-important interview or job offer, it should be the best you can make it.

The material in this book comes from years of helping health professionals, students, and trainees through the arduous task of writing résumés and personal statements. Many people spend long hours agonizing over the procedure, but end up with poor results. There is no reason for that. By following the guidelines in this book, anyone can prepare clearly written, succinct, and professional-looking materials for presentation to residencies, graduate training programs, potential employers, fellowships, and admissions/scholarship committees.

You may be like Mark, a second-year internal medicine resident who came into my office frustrated and bewildered. He had spent valuable hours preparing a résumé and personal statement to apply for a dermatology residency. After talking with him for five minutes and reading his documents, I immediately recognized that they did not reflect his accomplishments and strengths. We quickly revised his résumé and formulated a step-by-step approach that Mark used to write his personal statement. With this assistance he developed a clearly written and professional-looking application package that marketed his strengths. His self-confidence soared after he identified his strengths. Several months later, he returned to my office beaming. He had been offered a position with the dermatology program of his choice! He told me that he thought his résumé and personal statement had really opened some doors.

Your résumé and personal statement can open doors for you, too.

How to use this book

The book is divided into 12 chapters.

Chapter 1: Résumés and Personal Statements for Health Professionals: An Overview, describes how this book will help you prepare résumés and personal statements.

Chapter 2: What is a Résumé?, defines the term résumé (*curriculum vitae*) and answers such important questions about résumés as: Why do you need a résumé?; May you use "see résumé" on application forms?; What if you don't have enough experience to have a résumé?; What should you include in your résumé?; What should you omit?; What are some acceptable résumé formats and styles?; What are some résumé DOs and DON'Ts?; and, How do you print and mail your résumé?

Chapter 3: Your Personal Experience Inventory, uses a systematic approach to help you *recall* and *organize* your experiences, skills, and other valuable accomplishments so that you can present them in your résumé. The questionnaire is thorough–yet simple, painless, and easy to complete. Do you think that you haven't done anything worth putting in résumé? Think again. Completing the Personal Experience Inventory will provide you with the information to include in your résumé, as well as increased confidence in what you have accomplished.

Chapter 4: Writing Your Résumé: A Step-by-Step Plan, provides you with a step–by–step technique to write and revise your résumé. Each step is written to simplify the process, and assumes that you have no in-depth knowledge about writing résumés or using word processors. You can skip sections if you have experience with one or more of these areas. It also gives you time-saving suggestions to help you keep track of draft versions.

Chapter 5: Health Professionals' Résumés: Examples, contains numerous examples of health professionals' résumés. You'll see how different people in various health professions distilled and organized their experiences and marketable skills into their résumés. You'll learn how your résumé will be enhanced by selecting a style that reflects your personal tastes.

Chapter 6: What is a Personal Statement?, helps you develop a personalized marketing strategy that emphasizes key attributes desired by selection committees and employers. Are you struggling to communicate the experiences and events that shaped your personality, attitudes, values, and goals? This chapter will give you keen insight into how to get "you" across to others, and make them like you.

Chapter 7: Your Personal Marketing Inventory: Identifying Skills and Traits, helps you analyze your academic, extracurricular, and personal experiences. You'll learn to recognize skills and traits that reviewers seek and that make you unique.

Chapter 8: Developing Your Marketing Strategy, helps you match your skills and traits with qualifications that reviewers seek. You will discover that your strengths can literally match you to some programs or positions and, in some cases, keep you from matching with others. You will also learn to describe your strengths in terms that reviewers will understand.

Chapter 9: Writing Your Personal Statement: A Step-by-Step Plan, helps you fit your marketable skills onto a one-page personal statement. Since no "ideal" format exists, many people encounter "writer's block" when they sit down to write their personal statements. But here, you learn to help the reader come to know you as a person with desirable traits and interests. You'll also see that it's okay to take risks–to show the reader the "real" you.

Chapter 10: Health Professionals' Personal Statements: Examples, provides actual health professionals' personal statements to review. These personal statements are *different*: each depicts its author in a unique and personalized way. But the statements are similar, too, since they all let the reader "bond" with the writer *before* they ever meet in person. You'll get ideas for structuring your personal statement as you read these samples.

Chapter 11: Cover and Thank-You Letters, teaches you how to write winning cover and thank-you letters by providing guidelines for writing these important documents. It also contains some useful examples.

No, **Chapter 12: Building/Strengthening Your Résumé and Personal Statement,** doesn't contain quick and dirty hints to "pad" your résumé or personal statement. Instead, it gives you concrete strategies to prepare yourself for the future by developing certain skills today. It offers specific suggestions on how to actively work to enhance your strengths. This is an investment in the future for anyone entering undergraduate or professional school, or seeking career advancement.

Finally, the **Glossary** and **Annotated Bibliography** contain additional useful information to help you hone your résumé-writing and job-search skills.

This book emphasizes the idea that you should consider your current job or educational status as temporary. Keep your résumé up-to-date, and have one available when an opening presents itself. Carry several copies to professional conferences or meetings so you can share them with potential employers when unexpected opportunities arise. You say you don't want to change jobs? Even if you don't now, circumstances can change overnight. Be prepared!

2: What is a Résumé?

A polished résumé stands out from the crowd.

What is a résumé?

Résumé is a French word which means "summary." A Latin term which is often used interchangeably with it is *curriculum vitae* (abbreviated "CV"), meaning a short account of a person's career and personal qualifications. Thus, your résumé or CV summarizes your career and qualifications. The word "résumé" most commonly refers to a list of accomplishments and experiences for a job application, although in academic circles they more frequently use the phrase *curriculum vitae*. For consistency, in this book I will use the term résumé.

Your résumé tells admissions and selection committees, graduate training programs, and prospective employers who you are and what you have done, and suggests what your future potential might be. Most employers and selection committees can't interview everyone who applies for a position. They have to categorize people based on information in their application packets, and résumés are key parts of those packets. Reviewers create two piles of applications: those accepted for interviews and those rejected. Just two piles. Unfortunately, some of the applicants in the "reject" pile may have been qualified, but they failed to adequately market themselves to the initial reviewers. That's why polished résumés are so important. They help you get your foot in the door.

How should your résumé differ from a newspaper advertisement selling automobile tires? The tire ad is aimed at the general public. But your résumé is meant for a specific reader. Your résumé then, should emphasize specific experiences sought by that reader, who may be a prospective employer or admissions/selection committee, because he or she will use it to learn about you before meeting you in person. It has to be more than a mere listing of your job experiences. It must be interesting, informative, and easy to read. In short, it has to make the reader want to meet one of the most interesting people around–*you.*

Why do you need a résumé?

Even if you have a "dream" job now, it is likely that you'll apply for an even better position in the future. In a constantly changing career environment, résumés are essential. You need a résumé to

- apply for admission to a health professions program (schools of pharmacy, respiratory therapy, nursing, and osteopathic or allopathic medicine, etc.).

- apply for employment while you are in or after you have completed a health professions training program.

- apply for admission to a graduate program (e.g., M.P.H., Ph.D.).

- apply for many scholarships, loans, or grants.

- speak to groups. Someone needs to know what to say about you when introducing you to an audience.

- apply for a promotion. Many institutions include résumés as part of an individual's promotion portfolio.

Your résumé helps readers to *quickly* see that you have the knowledge, skills, experiences, and abilities they seek. Whether you apply for a training position, your first job, or a move up the ladder of success, a polished résumé creates a positive first impression and helps you get an interview.

You must ensure that your résumé reflects the particular experiences and skills, as well as education and training, that employers want. Don't assume that people will "read into" your experiences or hear about how great you are–even if you already work where you are applying. Here are two illustrations of how résumés opened doors for people just like you.

Diane, a life-long resident of Tucson, wanted to relocate to San Diego after graduating from the University of Arizona College of Nursing. Working part-time during nursing school and excelling in her courses and clinical rotations had given Diane an outstanding reputation in several Tucson hospitals. Her reputation resulted in three tempting job offers, but Diane wanted a change of scenery. Diane realized that she was an "unknown" in nursing circles in San Diego. So she invested considerable effort on her résumé, describing her experiences, skills, and abilities. The effort paid dividends: Diane was offered several positions, and she chose one that gave her an excellent salary, working conditions, and opportunities for professional growth.

Bruce, a medical technologist, earned an M.P.H. while working in a large hospital in Cleveland. When he applied for an administrative position in that same hospital, he initially spent little time on his résumé, believing that everyone there would know of him and his accomplishments. Bruce carefully prepared his résumé to show the administrators that he had the qualities they were seeking. This time, he got the position.

In short, health professionals like you need résumés. Unfortunately, some people don't realize that until it's too late, and they produce less-than-polished résumés.

John, a third-year medical student, rushed into my office. He said that he needed a résumé for a scholarship application. He had been procrastinating about completing the paperwork for nearly two months. The application was due in the Financial Aid office the next morning, and it had to be accompanied by a résumé that would "sell" him to the scholar-ship committee. He was alarmed, since he needed the scholarship money to eat during the next two months (when he wasn't eating hospital food). Using the guidelines in this book, we sat down together and wrote a polished résumé in about forty minutes. John was lucky that he had the resources to produce a résumé at the last moment. He had plenty of opportunities to write a résumé at less hectic times, but he just didn't do it.

Don't be like John. Plan and write your résumé *now*. Even if you don't have a deadline staring you in the face, you'll be ready to confront even the unforeseen when you hold a polished résumé in your hand!

What can a résumé do for you?

A polished résumé can do several things for you. Specifically, it can

- demonstrate your qualifications for a position.
- provide a written inventory of your marketable skills and experiences.
- reinforce your self-confidence.

- help you obtain interviews.

- remind you of your strengths immediately before an interview.

- organize your presentation during an interview.

- help you project a "can-do" attitude during the interview.

I can personally attest to the importance of résumés. In fact, I always carry several copies of my résumé when I attend national meetings, because you never know when a potential employer with an interesting opening might materialize. While attending a medical education conference, I just happened to join a small group session about student learning. During the session, representatives from two schools mentioned that they had just created the kind of position I wanted. Immediately after the session, I introduced myself to each person, handed them copies of my résumé, told them I was interested in their positions, and encouraged them to contact me. I received an interview and a job offer from each school.

It wasn't by accident that I had those résumés in my briefcase. Years before, I had realized that many positions are filled by personal contacts before they are advertised. So I started carrying several copies of my résumé when I traveled. After all, we never know who will sit next to us on a plane, in a restaurant, or at a workshop. Even if you really enjoy your current position, a better one might suddenly appear. Some people are ready for those "unexpected" opportunities. Make sure *you* are.

Can you use "see résumé" on application forms?

No.

Some companies, and most training programs, require people to complete their application forms to streamline and standardize application procedures. Many companies publish job announcements that list the **K**nowledge, **S**kills, and **A**bilities (KSAs) required for each advertised position. Personnel specialists (who often lack health care backgrounds) or screening panels (usually with some health care background) review all applications. They quickly scan these application forms for evidence of the KSAs described in the job announcement. They are accustomed to finding those KSAs in particular places on their forms. If they don't find something where they expect it to be, they rarely search for it. They seldom refer to other documents, like an applicant's résumé, to find missing information. In short, unless their KSAs are on the form, applicants don't get credit for having them. Those applications are placed in the "better-luck-next-time" pile.

Therefore, invest the time to *completely fill out all application forms*. Sure, it's a hassle and might duplicate what is on your résumé, but you have to play by the school's or company's rules if you want a chance at an interview. So, get the job announcement and application form(s), identify the required KSAs, and complete the form(s). Be sure to directly address each KSA. Type or print all information so reviewers can read it.

The only time to use "see résumé" is when you have *more* qualifications or information than will fit on an application form. In that case, the person screening your application will usually be pleased to look for the additional information.

A résumé can't guarantee that you'll get a specific job or that you'll be accepted into the program you want. There are plenty of well-qualified people in employment lines and program-applicant pools. But the reality is that the better you look on paper the greater the likelihood that you'll pass the initial screening.

What if you don't have enough experience to have a résumé?

I hear this comment often. Bright, successful people come into my office sighing that they have nothing to put in a résumé. They usually leave much happier after about twenty minutes, armed with the knowledge that they have the experiences needed to write an interesting résumé.

What happens during that twenty minutes? I go through the *Personal Experience Inventory* with them and help them focus on what they have done, instead of concentrating on what they haven't done.

People often overlook or undervalue their experiences. Even if you've been in school or out of the workforce for several years, you have gained marketable skills and knowledge. Leading community groups, tutoring adults or children, running for political office, learning word processing at home, working or volunteering in a hospital, supplying first-response health care, providing services to the disadvantaged, or volunteering at your place of worship all enhance your qualifications. The Personal Experience Inventory in Chapter 3 will help you identify the characteristics employers and selection committees seek in applicants. You may be pleasantly surprised when you identify skills and knowledge you never thought you possessed.

What should you include in your résumé?

You can include *anything* in your résumé that describes your marketable traits. Your résumé should detail the exact knowledge, skills, and abilities you possess and are desired by a prospective employer or selection committee. You need *not* have gained those qualifications in paid positions. So list any experience-building background, such as chairing a committee or organizing a neighborhood crime-watch group. Confused about what to include? As a general guideline, your résumé *can* include

- education.
- honors and awards.
- extracurricular activities.
- research experiences.
- specific clinical interests.
- licenses and certifications.
- languages you speak or write.
- publications or presentations to groups.
- membership in professional organizations.
- volunteer activities and personal interests.
- employment and teaching experiences.

You don't have to include every category of information in your résumé. In fact, few people–even Deans or hospital CEOs–include every category in their résumés. Chapters 3 and 4 will help you identify topics to include and show you the best way

9

to present them. Chapter 5 contains examples of actual résumés. Read these to see what others have done. (Many of the people who wrote those résumés originally thought that they didn't have enough material to fill a page.)

Caution: Don't be shy, but do avoid "padding" your résumé. Don't emulate comedians in stuffed sweatsuits who "pump up" in front of an audience. Just as you know the difference between real muscle and flab, so do most employers and admissions committees. An example of a "padded" résumé is one in which an applicant says he belongs to an organization, but, when pressed, admits he only attended one club meeting during the past three years. Another example is listing a publication when one's name does not appear on the list of authors. The excuse "I participated in the research, but somehow my name was omitted from the author list" doesn't work. If your name is missing, you can't count it as your publication. A "padded" résumé may make a person look good on paper, but there's little substance if anyone checks.

Should you include an "objective" section on your résumé?

Include an "objective" on your résumé only if it is *specific* and *matches the position* for which you are applying. For example, Barbara's objective initially read:

> I desire a challenging, professional position in nursing, focusing on holistic health.

Does Barbara's objective really describe the type of position she wants? I thought this objective was too general. It also is ambiguous–what exactly does she mean by 'holistic health'? Barbara and I discussed her nursing experience. She had worked in the emergency department and in cardiac rehabilitation, and her résumé displayed impressive specialized training and job skills in both areas. Barbara stated that she planned to apply for a newly created position in cardiac rehabilitation. Based on this, we revised her objective to read:

> A cardiac rehabilitation position in a large urban medical center.

Barbara's revised objective contains the words "cardiac rehabilitation" and "large urban medical center." These words specifically describe the type of position she wants. They also matched her to the position as it was advertised in the newspaper.

Lois, a dietitian, showed me her original objective for a position at another hospital.

> I am seeking a position in dietetics that complements my education and experience.

This objective is also too general and conveys no hint about which position she desires. Lois' revised objective is more focused.

> I seek a dietetics position in an urban hospital where I can use my clinical expertise to provide nutrition education and training to patients, their relatives, and hospital employees.

Notice how "urban hospital" and the emphasis on "clinical expertise to provide nutrition education" clearly indicate the job characteristics Lois desires. They also may be sought by potential employers.

Caution: A specific objective can *decrease* your chance of getting an interview if it contains words that do not match the available position. For example, if Barbara or Lois were applying for a position in a rural hospital, their objectives, as they appear above, would reduce their chances of obtaining an interview.

Therefore, if you include an objective on your résumé, be sure that it describes the type of position you want as well as the position that is being offered. Avoid words that will lower your chances of being interviewed at a place you might really like.

What are some résumé *DOs*?

I call the basic characteristics of effective résumés, "*Résumé DOs*" because your résumé should conform to them. Your résumé should be

- *short.* Most basic résumés should be one page so that they can be read in 20 seconds or less. Of course, you will have more pages if you have extensive employment or research experience. If your résumé is longer than one page, though, make sure you *put the most important information on the first page,* since there is no guarantee that the reviewer will read the second page.

- *honest.* Honestly describe what you have done. Don't exaggerate or inflate your responsibilities or duties.

- *actively written.* Use the action words in Figure 2.1 to describe your experiences. Avoid the passive voice. For example, instead of "Had responsibility for screening patients," write "Screened patients."

- *well-organized.* Make sure that readers can quickly and easily find the key information in your résumé–don't expect them to search.

- *readable.* Your résumé should be easy to read. Avoid small type (e.g., less than 10-point). Also, don't cram too much onto a page–leave some white space around the border.

- *organized to display important contact information.* Ensure that the reader can quickly find your name and contact information. Notice that the résumés in Chapter 5 contain Name and Address sections that are very easy to locate and read. I suggest you put your contact information at the top of the page. Highlight your name in boldface to make it more obvious, as shown.

Franklin C. Smith
6640 North Panama Lane
San Antonio, Texas 78213
210-555-6768

- *targeted to the needs of the reader.* If you know the requirements of a position, tailor your résumé to that job. This strategy helps readers recognize your experiences and skills that relate to the job they want to fill.

What are some résumé *DON'Ts*?

The "*résumé DON'Ts*" have no place in your résumé. Avoid these "*DON'Ts*" to save time, energy, and money–and maybe an interview. Your résumé must *not* contain

- *poor grammar.* Check your résumé for grammatical mistakes. Then ask a friend who is knowledgeable about grammar to check it again. Grammatical errors don't market your skills well.

- *spelling errors.* Don't just rely on a computer for this. Even spell-checking by computer has its limitations. First review the entire résumé and use a dictionary to recheck words that you question. Then ask a friend who can spell well to review it again.

- *inflated accomplishments.* Describe precisely the duties you performed in a position. Avoid using terms that exaggerate importance. For example, instead of "coordinated information distribution for a 10-person office," say "distributed mail and inter-office memos in a 10-person office."

- *deflated accomplishments.* Avoid the other extreme. Realistically describe your duties and accomplishments. A paid position isn't necessary to gain experience. Volunteers perform great services for others, while acquiring many skills. Don't sell yourself short.

What should you omit from your résumé?

While you may include many categories of information on your résumé, you should definitely omit some "personal" information because it could be a barrier to your selection or employment. Information that is obvious, extraneous, or confidential should also be omitted.

Federal and state equal employment opportunity laws make it illegal for employers to discriminate on the basis of gender, age, marital status, religion, race, creed, color, or physical disability. Some cities have laws protecting against discrimination based on sexual preference. Yet these laws are rarely enforced, even though many health professionals seeking positions report that they have experienced discrimination related to one or more of these factors. Of course, some information (e.g., age) can be determined based on data supplied on the résumé, but spelling it out directly is unwise.

A good guideline about personal information is this: Think before you include it in your résumé, and couch the information in such a way that you minimize any personal or negative biases. **Do not**

- *put the words "résumé," "curriculum vitae," or "CV" at the top of the page.* Employers and admissions/selection committees can usually spot a résumé from 100 meters. Leave "résumé" or "*curriculum vitae*" off and save a line.

- *include your Social Security number.* You can give the employer this information after you are hired.

- *mention your gender.* This can usually be determined from your name.

- *specify your age.* This can usually be determined from data you supply (e.g., graduation dates).

- *include the number of your professional license.* You can supply this confidential information later, if needed.

- *discuss your marital status.*

- *mention your health status or disabilities.* No résumé ever says a person is in "poor health." Only state that you are in "excellent health" *if the job requires it* and you *are* in excellent health. People hiring medical professionals are interested in knowing if applicants can do the job for which they are applying. Even if you are ill or disabled, do not include this personal information if you can do the job. If you will need special accommodations, extra or unusual times off, or help with doing the job, wait until after you have been offered the position to discuss these needs with the employer.

- *list your spouse's or significant other's name and age.* This information has absolutely nothing to do with your application for any position.

- *list your children's names and ages.* The same reasoning applies here. It might, be useful to include this information only for positions that require knowledge of, and experience with, children and adolescents.

- *list your height and weight.* This information is unnecessary for any civilian position in the medical professions. If you are entering the military, they will soon have that information–along with an assessment of your general physical condition.

- *include your race, ethnic background, or religion.* Federal and state equal employment opportunity laws make it illegal for employers to ask for this information. Don't include it on your résumé, unless it will increase your likelihood of getting a specific position.

- *discuss your availability or present/desired salary.* Negotiate availability and salary with your new employer *after* you have been offered the position

- *describe your willingness to relocate.* Include any information about your willingness to relocate in your cover letter when you apply for a position. For example, you can mention that your brothers now live in Baltimore and you would like to live closer to them. This information may vary with different applications.

- *list travel experiences.* List these only if they will help you get the position. For example, Frank traveled extensively in Central America and speaks Spanish fluently. Frank included this information when he applied for a hospital administrator's position in Brownsville, Texas.

Figure 2.1: Action Words

adapted	developed	introduced	recommended
adjusted	diagnosed	invented	recorded
administered	directed	investigated	recruited
advised	discovered	judged	reduced
analyzed	dispensed	launched	refined
approved	documented	lead	reorganized
arranged	drafted	lectured	replaced
assembled	edited	maintained	represented
assessed	educated	managed	researched
assisted	elected	marketed	restored
attained	eliminated	maximized	reviewed
audited	enhanced	measured	revised
authored	enlarged	minimized	saved
built	established	moderated	scheduled
calculated	evaluated	modernized	screened
chaired	examined	modified	selected
classified	exhibited	motivated	simplified
collected	expanded	negotiated	solved
communicated	fabricated	observed	spoke
compiled	facilitated	obtained	staffed
completed	formulated	operated	started
composed	founded	optimized	streamlined
conducted	gathered	orchestrated	strengthened
consolidated	generated	ordered	studied
constructed	governed	organized	suggested
consulted	guided	performed	summarized
contacted	handled	piloted	supervised
contributed	helped	pioneered	taught
controlled	hired	planned	televised
converted	illustrated	prepared	tested
coordinated	implemented	prescribed	trained
corrected	increased	presented	translated
counseled	inspected	presided	troubleshot
created	installed	programmed	tutored
demonstrated	instructed	provided	updated
designed	integrated	published	wrote
determined	interviewed	purchased	

- *describe why you left your last job.* Everyone changes positions for different reasons, but your résumé is not the place to discuss any of those reasons. Instead, be ready to answer this question during an interview.

- *enclose your photograph.* Under both Federal and most states' civil rights laws, it is illegal for a prospective employer to require or suggest that you supply a photograph. If however, you believe that your appearance might enhance your chances, include a photograph. Avoid "passport" photos from a machine. Invest in a professional portrait.

- *list references.* Your references will probably change when you apply for different types of positions. Your references may also change as you work with different people. This information also takes up too much valuable space on your résumé. If you must say something about references, write "excellent references available upon request." (I have never seen, however, "Poor references available upon request" on a résumé.) Have some excellent references lined up. It makes sense to form a network and maintain favorable ties with people who can act as references. When you are asked, you'll be able to supply prospective employers or admissions committees with great references. If references are specifically requested, supply them on a separate page attached to your résumé (so you can change it as needed). For each reference, include the person's full name, up-to-date contact information (e.g., telephone number), and a brief description of your relationship with that person. For example:

  > Gerald Brown, Ph.D., Professor, Department of Anatomy, Pritzker School of Medicine, University of Chicago, Chicago, IL 60637. Office telephone: 312-555-6707. Office Fax: 312-555-6709. Dr. Brown is the Medical Gross Anatomy course director. He supervised two anatomy electives I completed during my fourth year in medical school.

What are some acceptable résumé formats?

Acceptable résumés come in many styles. In fact, there is no "ideal" résumé format. Appearance does make a difference, as you will see when you compare Figures 2.2 and 2.3. Figure 2.2 is a first draft of a résumé. Figure 2.3 is the revised and edited version. (I prefer the format in Figure 2.3 because important information is easy to locate and read.) Note in Figure 2.3 that I followed the *Résumé DO*s and *DON'T*s described earlier. Other acceptable formats are shown in Chapter 5.

What are some acceptable levels of detail for résumés?

Résumés also contain various levels of detail, depending upon their intended use. Dale Townsend, an Associate Professor at a College of Pharmacy in the northwestern United States, has had a successful and highly productive career in both academics and private industry. She uses one of the following résumé styles, depending upon the situation.

- *Formal.* This style lists a person's lifelong accomplishments. It is the longest of the four types because it contains all information about a person's career. Dale's formal résumé is about seven pages long.

- *Focused.* This style, usually shorter than the formal format, accents a person's knowledge, skills, and abilities (KSAs) for a particular purpose (e.g., to apply for a position). It can be edited to include the accomplishments (e.g., publications or presentations) within a particular period (e.g., last ten years). Its contents can also be arranged to focus on specific skills. For example, Dale used the focused format to apply for positions in other pharmacy colleges. Dale's focused résumé for a faculty position would be worded and arranged differently than one for a position in private industry. Specifically, Teaching Experience/Awards are more highly valued in faculty positions than in research and development positions.

- *Abbreviated.* In this format, accomplishments are condensed and abbreviated to make the résumé easier to use, and to help the reader focus on particular issues. When speaking to community groups, Dale's abbreviated résumé provides the person who introduces her with an easy-to-use document that includes information she deems important. This format, however, prevents her from including the titles of all her publications. Instead, her one-page résumé condenses her publications (i.e., says "Published 63 articles in peer-reviewed journals.") and stresses that her major area of interest is poisonings among children.

- *Special.* These résumés follow guidelines established by others. Dale is about to apply for promotion to professor. Her college has a special format that dictates the accomplishments to be included and the way they should be arranged. The college also requires her to list such things as "percentage of effort" on a publication–information not required in other résumé formats. In fact, many universities are now switching to unique and specific formats for résumés.

Should you use a computer-generated résumé?

Yes! Use a computer to write your résumé. It's a waste of time to type it on a standard typewriter. (Not to mention the toxic levels of correction fluid that may accumulate in your bloodstream!) A computer-generated résumé allows you to save the file, correct errors, and easily update it when needed. Computers are the way to go! Even if you consider yourself "computer illiterate," it takes only a few minutes to get started in a Windows™ or Macintosh™ word processing program.

While any word processing program can produce an acceptable résumé, some programs now have built-in résumé templates. The program I use (Microsoft® Word 6.0) allows me to select from among several templates that I can easily tailor to my needs. To use these templates, I simply type over the information the program presents (e.g., when it shows a date, I type the appropriate date in the designated area). Other word processing programs, such as WordPerfect® 6.0 also have this feature. Check your program's documentation to determine if it has résumé templates. If it does, experiment to see if you like the format and style of the résumés

Figure 2.2: A "Before" Résumé (First Draft)

<u>Curriculum Vitae</u>
Ted P. Gregory
6784 South Crestline Ave.
Tucson, Arizona 85733

<u>Personal Information</u>
SSN: 123-45-6789; DOB: March 20, 1967; Health: Excellent
Marital Status: Married to Kyle for 3 years, 2 children

<u>Education</u>   College of Medicine Univesrity of Arizona,
            Tucson, Arizona, Doctor of Medicine, 1994
                Brodie College, May 1990, *summa cum laude*
        Yuma, Arizona. Zoology Major
        Arizona Central High School, June 1, 1986
                Canyon, Arizona

    <u>Honors/Awards</u>
    Honorsin Bio-chemistry and Intrenal Medicine
        John P. Sacks Award, 1990
    Harvill Scholraship, 1986 to 1990
    Phi Beta Kappa, 1990

<u>Extracuricular Activities</u>
        Athletic Booster Club President, 1989-90
                Pre-Med Club, 1989
        Research with Dr. Clemans, 1991

<u>Clinical Intreests</u>
    cardiovascular system

            <u>Volunteer Activities</u>
Volunteer, Canyon Hospital, Canyon, AZ, 1984
Emergency Department, University Medical Center, 1991

        <u>Employment Experience</u>
Nursing Assistant, Canyon Hospital, AZ, 1984-1986

Professional Organizations
    American Medical Association, 1990-Present

<u>Language</u>   Spanish

<u>Personal Interests</u>   Exercise, reading, cooking, cars

Figure 2.3: An "After" Résumé (Final Draft)

Ted P. Gregory
6784 S. Crestline Ave.
Tucson, AZ 85733
602-555-9898

Education	M.D.	University of Arizona College of Medicine, 1994 Tucson, AZ
	B.S.	Brodie College, 1990 Yuma, AZ Major: Zoology, graduated *summa cum laude*

Honors and Awards

Medical School
  Honors earned in Internal Medicine and Biochemistry
  John P. Sacks Award for Excellence in Anatomy, 1990
Undergraduate
  Phi Beta Kappa, 1990
  Harvill Academic Scholarship (tuition), 1986-90
  Top Chemistry Major, Brodie College, 1990

Research Experience

HSV-I Mutants Resistant to 2'-nor-deoxy-guanosine,
  with S. Clemans, Ph.D., University of Arizona,
  Biochemistry Dept., 1991

Extracurricular Activities

Undergraduate School
  Pre-Med Club, 1988-90; President, 1990
  Athletic Booster Club, 1986-90; President, 1989-90

Language Skills   Spanish

Volunteer Activities   Emergency Department, University Medical Center, 1991

Employment Experience

Emergency Department Assistant, Canyon Hospital
  Canyon, Arizona, 1985-86

Nursing Assistant, Canyon Hospital, Canyon, Arizona, 1984

Organization   American Medical Association, 1990-Present

Personal Activities   Biking, reading "Old West" books, Oriental cooking,
  restoring antique automobiles

it offers. If you are an intermediate-level word processing user, design a template to your own specifications. Again, check the résumés in Chapter 5 to see what you like and adapt the style and format to your needs.

Commercially available programs especially designed to produce résumés are also available. They are quick and easy to use. Read their documentation to see if you like their styles and formats.

Chapter 4 contains additional hints on using computers.

What types of printers are acceptable?

Use either a laser or ink-jet printer. They both provide an array of fonts and type sizes, and the quality is impressive. Check your word processing program and printer to determine the choices you have. I use Microsoft® Word 6.0 and a Hewlett-Packard LaserJet III™. This combination, besides its numerous options for type styles, also allows me to print in fractional parts of a point (e.g., 10.5). (This option is important when you have a lot to get on a page, but you don't want it to appear crowded.) Some font styles and sizes are shown in Figure 2.4.

As Figure 2.4 illustrates, the font and point size used can affect your résumé's readability and the amount of material you can put on a page. Avoid a font that is difficult to read, and avoid a point size that can only be seen with the aid of a magnifying glass.

Don't print your résumé on a dot-matrix printer. Even the best content can be overlooked if the printing quality is poor. However, don't buy a printer especially for your résumé. Most local print or quick-copy shops will print your résumé and other application materials on a cost-per-page basis. If you are in school, ask about your institution's microcomputer facilities. Most schools now have microcomputers available in laboratories or libraries.

What kind of paper should you use?

The "eye appeal" of a résumé is important. Print your résumé on quality paper, such as 25% cotton bond. The contrast between the paper and print, coupled with the "feel" of the paper will separate your résumé from the ones that are printed on standard white paper. Most applicants will want to select neutral colors (like beige), avoiding "loud" colors. Some of these "loud" colors may create a negative impression, and you don't know the reviewers' preferences. In addition, many companies distribute photocopies to reviewers, so only secretaries see the original applications and letters before they are photocopied for distribution and then filed as a data base. Some paper colors (e.g., dark blue) will not copy well due to poor print to paper contrast. However, if you like a distinctive color, print your résumé on it and make a photocopy to check its quality. If it makes a good copy and fits your style, *go for it!*

Buy quality paper from a paper store or print shop. Compare prices for the amount and type of paper you need. Paper stores usually have a better selection, and may be less expensive than print shops.

Avoid fancy and expensive binders. Employers are more concerned about what is *in* a résumé than how it is packaged. Anyway, a clerk usually removes résumés from their binders for photocopying, so they aren't a good investment.

Figure 2.4: Examples of Font Styles and Point Options

Font	10 Point	12 Point
Arial Narrow™	Health Professional	Health Professional
Arial™	Health Professional	Health Professional
CASTELLAR™	HEALTH PROFESSIONAL	HEALTH PROFESSIONAL
Courier	Health Professional	Health Professional
Peignot Medium™	Health Professional	Health Professional
Baskerville Oldface™	Health Professional	Health Professional
Eurostile™	Health Professional	Health Professional
Century Gothic™	Health Professional	Health Professional
Times New Roman™	Health Professional	Health Professional

How should you package and mail your résumé?

Mail your résumé in a large envelope that can hold it without folding. If you must get your résumé to someone fast, you may send it as a Fax. If you fax it, though, immediately mail an original version to the recipient. Other ways to send résumés rapidly include Federal Express, United Parcel Service, and the U.S. Postal Service's two-day letter (priority mail) service. This latter option includes a large cardboard envelope and costs $2.90 (in 1994).

Should you enclose a cover letter with your résumé?

Although you don't *have* to enclose a cover letter (see Chapter 11) with every résumé you send, it is a good idea to include one. A well-written cover letter allows you to introduce yourself and share some personal information that does not appear on your résumé. For example, Michelle, a respiratory therapist who lived in Norfolk, Virginia, wanted to relocate to Madison, Wisconsin, so that she could be closer to her parents. When applying for a position in Madison, Michelle used her cover letter to express her interest in the position and to explain her motivation for wanting to relocate. The screening committee noted that Michelle's résumé documented the knowledge, skills, and abilities required in the position, and her cover letter helped them understand why she wanted a similar position in a different state.

Should you use a professional résumé writer?

Maybe. If you have more money than time, consider using the services of a professional résumé writer. Professional résumé writers, who charge to assist you in designing your résumé, ask you questions similar to those in the Personal Experience Inventory (Chapter 3) to delineate your experiences. They then distill those experiences on to the written page using a résumé style you select from among a group of options. After you approve the draft, they print the final version and give you the original and a specified number of copies. They usually charge $25 to $150 for this. Most do great-looking work, and if you are pressed for time you might want to use their services. Before you purchase their services, though, "comparison shop" among several professional résumé writers. If their services are beyond your budget, ask a secretary or secretarial service to prepare your résumé on a computer. They will often cost much less than using a résumé professional. If you can provide the content, a secretary can produce a style and format (and often help with proofreading) with your guidance.

The electronic future

In the future, residency and employment applications will take advantage of technology (and, hopefully, save a forest). Two items most medical professionals need to be aware of are scanners and the Electronic Residency Application Service (ERAS).

Many institutions, and especially larger corporations, now scan résumés, personal statements, and applications into computers so that many people can access and review them from their computer screens. At present, however, few applicants to health professions schools, graduate programs, residencies, or clinically based positions will encounter this practice. In general, medicine and academia have not yet discovered how small computers and networks can benefit them. If you believe your material will be electronically scanned, follow the recommendations below.

The Electronic Residency Application Service (ERAS), a joint project of the Association of American Medical Colleges and the American Medical Association, will likely be fully implemented by the late 1990s. It will allow residency applicants to enter their data on a disk which they will send to a central location for distribution to the programs they select. ERAS will allow students to tailor their applications by entering a different personal statement for each program, if they wish.

Such an electronic data base will likely allow applicants to "scan" their personal statements directly into the system. The following guidelines will facilitate this scanning process.

- Check with a local computer expert to identify the best hardware and software to use to scan your personal statement.

- Use plain, type-written text. TimesRoman™ is an excellent font to use.

- Eliminate any underlining, bold type, and italics, since most computer scanners cannot recognize these variations.

- Avoid multiple columns (software may have difficulty with multiple columns).

- Avoid graphics (current software cannot deal well with graphics).

- Avoid accent marks (e.g., é, ŏ, û, ñ) and special characters (e.g., ©, ®, ç, æ) because they will not scan well.

Now, on to the Personal Experience Inventory!

Your basic questions about résumés should be answered. It is time to assess your experiences to decide what you should put in your résumé. This process will take you less than thirty minutes, but it's a wonderful investment of your time. After you complete the inventory you should be able to quickly translate the ideas you have generated into a polished résumé. Now, enjoy the Personal Experience Inventory.

3: Your Personal Experience Inventory

Take stock of your experiences before you write.

What is a Personal Experience Inventory?

You've done so much in your lifetime. Your experiences influenced your development as a health care professional and person. You now have to recall those that employers and selection committees need to know. You must also organize them for your résumé. That's the purpose of the Personal Experience Inventory.

The Inventory is painless and easy to complete. If you have had relevant experience in a category (e.g., Education), simply list your experiences. (Yes, remembering the correct dates for some of your activities might take some brain work.) This information, however, is important–you'll use it to write your résumé in Chapter 4. Use additional paper if necessary. In fact, it is a good idea to buy a notebook and reserve several pages for each category. Then you can easily add new experiences in the future.

YOUR PERSONAL EXPERIENCE INVENTORY

Instructions: A list of categories is provided below. In front of each category is a box ☐. For each category, check the box (☑) if you have relevant experience in that area. Then honestly and accurately detail your experiences so that you can insert them into your résumé later. Few people have entries in every category–don't worry about that. At this stage, *include everything you have ever done*. You can edit some of it out later, if necessary.

☐ Education

List, in reverse chronological order (last to first), all the undergraduate, professional, and graduate schools you have attended. Include the degree earned (if any) and the date granted or dates attended, the institution, location (city and state), and your major/minor areas of study.

	Institution	Location	Dates	Degree/Area
Fellowship				
Fellowship				
Graduate School				
Graduate School				
Professional School				
Professional School				
Undergraduate School				
Undergraduate School				
Undergraduate School				
High School*				

* Only list "High School" if that has been your highest education level.

☐ Honors and Awards

List all honors, awards, or special recognition you have received from schools or other organizations. List any academic recognition received for a high grade-point average, such as Phi Beta Kappa, Alpha Omega Alpha, Phi Kappa Phi, etc. Include "honors" grades in courses or clinical clerkships, listing the clerkships first. List academic scholarships and special awards. Describe the honor if its title does not make its significance obvious. For example:

Instead of : George Anderson Memorial Medal

Write: George Anderson Memorial Medal for Academic Excellence

Honor/Award	Organization Giving Honor/Award	Date

❏ Extracurricular Activities

Detail all extracurricular activities to which you have devoted substantial time. Record memberships in clubs, organizations, service groups, and committee positions, etc. *Don't* include activities of very short duration (e.g., attended one meeting of a club). Include the dates you participated and any special positions you held. If the main purpose of the activity is not apparent from the name, briefly describe it.

Activity	Position/Description	Dates

☐ Research Experiences

Describe all research projects in which you have been involved. Perhaps you worked in a lab doing bench research like Roberta, now a third-year medical student, or assisted in a clinical study during your training, like Max, who is applying for his first nursing position. You may have even designed and run your own research like Lee, who is a practicing dentist seeking a position on the faculty of the School of Dentistry. Record your research experience *even if no publication or presentation resulted.* Write down your duties–be specific–e.g., "Surveyed patients in dermatology clinic," or "Analyzed cost-benefit data in a five-hospital system." If *you* received funding for the research, list the amount, dates, and source.

Project Title/Description	Site/Research Supervisor/Funding	Dates

❑ Publications

List the title, journal, publication data, and authors directly from each article. Include the chapter title, book title, and publisher information for texts. When you list publications in your résumé, use **boldface** or underlining to emphasize your name if there is more than one author. To remember this, it is probably a good idea to do it now. An example is provided.

Authors	Title	Journal/Book	Date;Volume:page
Sherk M, Galen P, Andrew, RI Larry SI,	Clinical decisions at the end of life	*International Ethics*	1994; 38:28-34

☐ Presentations

List the presentation's title, the organization or group who composed the audience, the location, and date. Do *not* include class presentations (e.g., when you presented a patient case in biochemistry or a patient-care plan to your clinical practice group). See the example.

Title	Audience	Place/Date
Advance Directives: Living Wills and Health Care Directives	Annual Health Care Forum: Nursing, medical, pastoral care, students, and social service staff	University Medical Center, New York, NY; January 3, 1994

❑ Clinical Interests

What are your current clinical interests? If you are an experienced health care professional, are you an expert in any specific area? You may have had special clinical training, or you might just have a keen interest in a particular subject. You don't have to have conducted research, published an article, or made a presentation on the topic. Perhaps you are a student and this area has always intrigued you and even stimulated you to read about it on your own beyond the scope of course assignments. Note that the table includes a "Background/Expertise" section to help you determine if you have genuine interest or a passing attraction for a topic. You won't actually list "Background/Expertise" on your résumé, but you may discuss this in subsequent interviews. But describe it now as you list your interests and expertise. Be specific, i.e., list "cystic fibrosis" rather than "pediatric illnesses."

Clinical Interest	Background/Expertise
Emphysema	Favorite uncle has emphysema/read journals and texts

❑ Volunteer Activities

Describe your volunteer activities (work *without* pay). Include organizations/groups to which you have donated your time, their location (city and state), your title (if any), and dates. Describe the organization's purpose if it is not obvious. Also list your major duties. An example is provided.

Organization	Duties	Place	Dates
Southern Arizona Rescue Association (volunteer search and rescue. Averages 1.5 calls/week)	Field member. Conduct mountain, desert, cave, and river searches and rescues. On-call by pager 24-hours/day. President 1989-91.	All of southern Arizona, occasionally in New Mexico and Mexico.	1981 to Present.

☐ Teaching Experiences

List any teaching or tutoring experience. Specifically cite your position, your subject or content area, the audience (i.e., people taught or tutored), the institution, location, and dates of service. (Some of these may be duplicated elsewhere.) An example is provided.

Position/Dates	Subject/Content	Audience	Institution/Location
Instructor 1992-Present	Basic Life Support (CPR)	High school students, their parents, and teachers	San Francisco, CA and Palo Alto, CA

❑ Employment Experiences

Describe your employment activities (work *with* pay). Include your titles (if any), the organizations for whom you worked, their location (city and state), and the dates of your service. Describe your major duties using the Table of Action Words in Chapter 2. (Also put in your supervisor's name while you are thinking about it. You may want this information later for reference letters.) For military service, include the service branch, rank on discharge, specialty, type of discharge (only if Honorable), and dates. An example is provided.

Position Title	Organization/Location	Duties	Dates
Patient Care Technician	Emergency Department, Beth Israel Hospital, Boston, MA	Draw blood, do EKGs, scribe for trauma cases, perform numerous nursing functions.	1991-93

❑ Licenses and Certifications

Nurses, pharmacists, physicians, podiatrists, dentists, and other health care professionals must hold state *licenses* to practice. List any license(s) you hold, their numbers, the issuing states, and the expiration dates, if applicable. *Certifications* come in two forms: *permits to practice,* such as for emergency medical technicians (EMTs), radiology technicians, or physical therapists, and recognition of *passing special examinations,* such as the ECFMG (for international medical graduates), USMLE (for physicians–also the old NBME "boards" or the FLEX), state nursing board examinations, national registry (Medical Technologist), or any of the special short-courses, such as Advanced Cardiac Life Support (ACLS), or Pediatric Advanced Life Support (PALS). List *all* current certifications. If they are directly relevant to the position you seek, also list prior certifications, such as listing an expired EMT certification when applying for a position as a health-professions student. *Do not* list the license or certification numbers on your résumé for security reasons. (But your private list can be a great reference tool when you fill out the myriad of forms at a new job or for a license or certification in another state.) An example is provided for each.

Type of License/Cert.	State Issued	Number	Expiration Date
Physician	Arizona	ZZ-99999	January 1, 1996
Paramedic	New York	PM-99999	January 1, 1998

❑ Languages

List any languages other than English (e.g., Spanish, French, etc.) that you can speak or write. You don't have to speak the language fluently to claim it, but you should be able to conduct a basic conversation using it. Descriptors for fluency include "native," "fluent," "intermediate," or "basic/rudimentary." If your name or background might indicate that English is not your first language, list English and specify your fluency in each category.

Language	Spoken	Written	Reading

☐ Professional Organizations

List all professional organizations (e.g., ANA, ADA, ASHP, AMA, etc.) to which you currently belong. Include student and resident memberships. Use the *full name* of the organization, and indicate any leadership positions you have held. An example is provided.

Organization	Positions	Dates
American Medical Student Association (AMSA)	School representative, 1994-95	1993-Present

☐ Personal Interests

List your interests and hobbies. Sally, a family medicine resident, is an avid runner. Perhaps you climb mountains, swim, ski, or play tennis or softball. Perhaps you restore antique automobiles or build furniture. Record those types of interests here. You can include "family" as an interest, but *don't* list the names of your spouse, significant other, or children.

_____

_____

_____

_____

_____

_____

_____

_____

Finished with the Personal Experience Inventory?

Congratulations! You've done the hardest part of preparing a résumé! Now that you have listed your experiences, all you have to do is organize them in a résumé format. Chapter 4 will show you how to do that quickly and easily. In no time at all you will have a polished résumé!

4: Writing Your Résumé: A Step-by-Step Plan

Steps to a polished résumé.

Use a step-by-step approach to prepare your résumé

This chapter gives you a step-by-step technique to write your résumé. Each step is written to simplify the process and assumes that you have no in-depth knowledge about writing résumés or using word processors. You can combine or skip steps if you have experience in one or both of these areas. Check off each step as you complete it. Most steps, like "Review other résumés," can be *accomplished* quickly. Other steps, such as "Print a draft copy of your résumé," will *happen* quickly (assuming you have no glitch in your computer/printer setup). The last step is the most fulfilling–printing your final version, after which you can submit your application package with confidence.

Materials needed

You'll need the materials below to complete your résumé. It's a good idea to read over the list before you begin writing. You probably have most of them in or on your desk.

- This book (read Chapters 2 to 5).

- Completed Personal Experience Inventory (Chapter 3).

- A computer disk formatted for the computer you'll use.

- Computer with word processing software.

- Laser or ink-jet printer.

- Plain printer paper.

- Résumé quality paper (from a local paper store or print shop).

If you don't have access to a computer or do not feel comfortable using one, you should complete your résumé in hand-written form. You will need to arrange for someone–a friend, secretary, or a commercial agency–to do the word processing. If you have a computer, but not a printer, arrange to use a printer that is compatible with your computer and word processing program. Many commercial print shops, libraries, and schools have printers available on a "fee-per-page" basis. Try out the printer you plan to use *in advance* to insure compatibility and readability.

STEPS IN PREPARING A RÉSUMÉ

☐ 1. ***Review other résumés.*** Scan the résumé examples in Chapter 5 to get ideas about what to include in your résumé and how to arrange the information. Also, notice that in some ways these résumés are all alike. They all contain the same basic information such as Education, Honors and Awards, etc. Yet each is different, reflecting the author's unique experiences and personal style.

☐ 2. ***Review your completed Personal Experience Inventory.*** Check your inventory (Chapter 3) for accuracy and completeness. You don't want to forget something important! You'll need that information so that you or someone else can enter it on the word processor. Check especially for correct dates. If you don't have this information and you will be using an office or school computer, you will have to make a trip home to retrieve some information or delay finishing your first draft.

☐ 3. ***Select the categories of information to include on your résumé.*** List each category you want to include. Examples of categories frequently contained on résumés include Education, Honors and Awards, and Personal Interests. Many health professionals' résumés also contain categories such as Languages and Research Experience. Be sure, each time you write a résumé, to tailor these so that they are relevant to the position you seek. However, *don't be disappointed* if you lack experience in every category. (If your résumé includes every category, think about applying for a Dean or CEO position!) The list should appear something like the one below.

__	Contact Information	__	Licenses
__	Education	__	Certifications
__	Honors and Awards	__	Languages
__	Employment Experiences	__	Clinical Interests
__	Research Experiences	__	Professional Organizations
__	Teaching Experiences	__	Extracurricular Activities
__	Publications	__	Volunteer Activities
__	Presentations	__	Personal Interests

❑ **4.** *Number the categories in the order you want them to appear on your résumé.* Note that except in rare instances, Education will always be the first or second category on a résumé. Students may put work experience low on their lists, but once you are working as a health professional, the Employment Experiences category should be placed close to the top of your résumé.

❑ **5.** *Select a résumé format.* There is no single best résumé format. An acceptable format allows the reader to quickly scan the page to identify key information. Employers and selection committee members don't like to search for information, so use a format that is well-organized and has ample "white space." Avoid cramming words into every available spot. Leave margins of at least 0.8 inches wide on all sides. Use a type size of 10 points or larger to make the print easier to read. Likewise, check your word processing program and printer to determine the font styles (e.g., Swiss or Times New Roman) available. Print your résumé in several of the fonts to identify those most easily read. Arial Narrow or Times New Roman are examples that are readable and conserve space. `Avoid Courier type (like this sentence) because it takes up too much space and looks like standard typewriter type.`

Remember that the format may depend upon why you need a résumé. You might try several formats and type styles to see which is the best for you.

❑ **6.** *Prepare a draft version of your résumé.* Include the categories and specific information as suggested below, based on the format you select. Arrange the categories in your own résumé, however, in the order you selected in Step 4 above. Remember to refer to Figure 2.1 for ideas to enliven the descriptions. Be sure to tailor all information to the desired position and institution. Each résumé you write may be different in some way, whether in the order of or emphasis placed on items.

Contact Information

The first information in your résumé should be your name, address(es) and telephone number(s). Put them at the top of the page, and be sure that they *stand out from the rest of the text*. If you will be traveling or moving, remember to include all the addresses (and dates that they apply) where you can be contacted. You don't want to miss out on a great position because the employer fails to reach you. If necessary, arrange for someone to take messages and forward them to you.

Education

Degree   Institution, Year of Graduation (do not include month)
            City and State of school
            Major/Minor

List all schools in *reverse* chronological order (most recent first). Use your judgment about how far back you should list your schools. Most people who apply for jobs after their professional education (including medical residencies and clinical nursing fellowships) do not include the high school from which they graduated. Examples are shown below.

M.D.   Georgetown University School of Medicine, 1994
          Washington, D.C.
M.S.   University of Cincinnati, 1990
          Cincinnati, Ohio
          Molecular and Cellular Biology
B.S.   University of Chicago, 1988
          Chicago, Illinois
          Biology

If you haven't completed your degree, write "anticipated" in parentheses following the month and year of your planned graduation.

B.S.N.   University of Maryland School of Nursing
          May 1995 (anticipated)
          Baltimore, Maryland

If you attended a school, but did not graduate (and do not anticipate graduating) from that institution, include that education as follows:

M.D.   University of Texas Medical School at Galveston, 1994
          Galveston, Texas
          Texas Tech University School of Medicine, 1990-92
          Lubbock, Texas

Honors and Awards

List any significant honors, awards, or special recognition you have earned. You may, of course, include any honor or award you have received, but use your common sense. Don't list high school honors (except valedictorian or National Merit Scholarship recipient). List only merit-based scholarships. Explain the award if the reader might have difficulty understanding why it was presented, or from whom you received it. For example,

> Instead of: Fred C. Smith Award

> Write: Fred C. Smith Award (junior chemistry major with highest grade-point average)

Be sure you list these awards in an order that catches the reader's attention–not necessarily in the order in which you earned them. Generally, list any nationally recognized (in your profession) awards first, such as induction into your profession's honor society. Then list school and local awards. Within each subgroup, you should list your most recent awards first. Some individuals list dates, others don't.

Include "honors" earned in courses (e.g., biochemistry) in the order that they relate to the position you seek. For a medical residency application, list honors in clinical courses first, focusing on the specialty for which you are applying (e.g., if you are applying for an emergency medicine residency, list emergency medicine electives and then clerkships such as surgery and internal medicine). The résumé's Honors and Awards section from an applicant for a pediatric residency might look like this:

- AOA (National Honor Society)

- Honors earned in Pediatrics, Internal Medicine, and Biochemistry

Research Experience

You probably learned a great deal about some topic–and the research process itself–if you participated in a research project. List your experience *even if no publication or presentation ever resulted from the project.* List your most recent experience first. For example:

- Children's Dental Awareness Study. Surveyor and primary data analyst under Rosa Villar, D.M.D., Department of Public Health Dentistry, University of Maryland School of Dentistry, Baltimore, Maryland, Summer 1994

Extracurricular Activities

List extracurricular activities in reverse chronological order. Include clubs, service organizations, committees, and sports activities. Give the dates you participated and any special offices you held or duties you performed. Again, use your common sense. I suggest you *not* include short-duration activities (e.g., leading one group of applicants around your school for an hour) because an interviewer might ask you to explain what you did in that activity. Here is one example of an Extracurricular Activities section:

Commitment to Underserved People, 1990-94 (*months aren't necessary*)
    Refugee Clinic Translator
Interaction Ministries, 1987-90
    Missions Coordinator, 1988-89
Student Exchange Summer Program, Bolivia, 1988

Evaluate each group you list. Remember that listing certain groups can open *or* close doors of opportunity. Listing some religious or radical groups to which you have belonged may give some readers a negative impression. However, include such memberships on your résumé if you are adamant about disclosing this information. (I believe that if someone has a problem with your group memberships, you want to know it early–before they hire you–rather than after you've been on the job for a month.)

Publications

List any publications on which you are included as an author, putting the most recent first. Include the title, journal name, publication data, and authors for each journal article. Include text title, chapter title, authors/editors, and publication data for books or other scholarly works. You may put these in any acceptable standard format used in your profession. It is best to use the bibliographic format from the major professional journal in your discipline. Notice that the résumé writer's name (Roy Andrews) is underlined or boldfaced–always a good practice if there is more than one author.

- Sherk M, Galen P, <u>Andrews RI</u>, Larry SI: Clinical decisions at the end of life. *International Ethics*, 1994:38:28-34

Applicants with many publications should divide them into groups in this order: books, refereed publications (including editorials and published abstracts), and non-refereed publications.

Presentations

Include presentations you have given to local, regional, or national professional groups. List the presentation title and meeting information, including the organization, city, and date. (See the example below.) Again, evaluate each presentation you list on your résumé. Don't list local presentations (e.g., noon conferences) to small groups of people. For example, I don't list résumé preparation workshops to groups of medical, nursing, or pharmacy students on my résumé. A smart reader can detect this "padding."

"Advance Directives: Living Wills and Health Care Directives," Annual Health Care Forum, University Medical Center, New York, NY, January 1994.

Clinical Interests

List *specific* clinical interests that may grab the attention of someone on the selection committee or interviewing panel. The interests cited should relate to the job. Consider these examples.

Nurse: Critical care nursing, especially with cardiac and cardiovascular surgery patients.

Physician: Child/Adolescent Psychiatry with focus on psychotherapy and psychopharmacology.

Dentist: Pediatric and adolescent dentistry–acute and preventative care.

Licenses

List all current licenses (e.g., M.D., R.N.) you hold, and the state where each was issued. Include the expiration dates, if applicable. List the most advanced licenses first. If they are relevant to the position you seek, put your expired licenses last. For security reasons, *do not* include your license numbers.

- P.A., Texas, expires July 1997

Certifications

Cite all currently held certifications (e.g., USMLE, ACLS, PALS, National EMS Registry, NBEOPS) including the states where they were issued and their expiration dates, if any. For security reasons, omit the certificate numbers. List the most advanced certifications first.

- M.T. (ASCP), expires January 1997
- Advanced Cardiac Life Support, expires June 1996

Languages

List languages you are familiar with other than English. Specify written or verbal proficiency. Use your judgment. You don't have to speak a language fluently to claim it. However, you should be able to conduct a basic conversation in the language. If you are *not* a native English speaker, you may want to affirm that you are fluent in written and conversational English. One caveat, however. Avoid listing a language you don't want to use, or if you *hate* to translate, because your employer might assume that you will voluntarily act as a translator for others and will expect you to do so.

- Intermediate-level French, written & spoken
- Basic German, written

Professional Organizations

List the professional groups with which you are currently affiliated. Note the dates you participated and any special duties you had. If you were an officer or committee chair, include this information with the dates you served. Student and resident memberships *do* count and should be listed. Do *not* use abbreviations in your résumé. What, for example, does ADA mean? The American Dietetic Association, the American Dental Association, or any one of a dozen other groups with those initials? Spell it out! Also, if the name of an organization does not clearly indicate its purposes, describe its professional importance. Examples are shown below.

- Student National Medical Association (SNMA), 1993-Present
  School representative, 1994-95

- California Nurses Association, 1993-Present

Teaching Experiences

Describe your teaching experiences. List the subjects taught, grade levels of students, dates, and locations. If you have very specialized skills and they are relevant, mention them.

- Instructor, Wilderness Emergency Care, National Ski Patrol members,
  Colorado Springs, CO, 1993-95

Volunteer Activities

Describe your volunteer experiences. State the organization's name, its location, and your dates of service. If space is available, *briefly* list your major duties. Be sure that there is enough of a description, however, to get the point across and to pique the reader's interest. (Avoid a lengthy listing of your duties.) Remember to spell out the organization's purpose if it is not obvious from its name or if it is a relatively unknown group.

Note that as with the sections on Extracurricular Activities and Professional Organizations, referring to religious or political activities may either help or harm your application–depending on the prejudices of the reviewers. If you don't feel strongly about listing something, remember the caveat: *When in doubt, leave it out.*

- Alpha Phi Omega (national fraternity for volunteer service), 1987-92

- Southern Arizona Rescue Association (volunteer wilderness search and rescue–average 1.5 calls/week). Field member, on-call for mountain, cave, and river searches and rescues. Based in Tucson, AZ, covers southern AZ and adjacent areas. 1981-Present

Employment Experiences

Describe your employment experiences. State job titles, the names of the organizations or companies, their locations (city and state), and your dates of employment. Avoid a lengthy listing of your duties. If space is available, *briefly* list your major duties. The strongest listings include those directly related to the position for which you are applying. Other strong listings are those in health-related jobs. Of course, if you are just beginning your career, nearly any employment will be viewed more favorably than none at all. Note the difference between the strong and weak listings in the following examples.

- Patient Care Technician, Emergency Department, Beth Israel Hospital, Boston, MA, 1991-93. Performed many bedside nursing functions, including blood draws and EKGs.   (*STRONG* listing)
- Golf caddie, Framingham Country Club, Framingham, MA, 1988-90.
(*WEAK* listing)

Personal Interests

List your hobbies and things you like to do outside of the health care arena. List activities that might "stick" to the readers' minds or that are related to the position you seek. Cooking (specify type), woodworking, hockey, hiking, snow skiing, ice-skating, tennis, jogging, reading, and restoring furniture or antique automobiles are some interests I have seen on résumés. Listing "family" is okay, but don't include your spouse's, significant other's, or children's names. In fact, *omit* this entire section if its contents are unlikely to match the interests of the readers or if your résumé is already strong or too long.

☐ **7. *Give your résumé an understandable file name when you save it on your computer disk.*** Instead of a file name like "CV" or "résumé," name the file so that you can find it quickly and easily. For example, your file name can contain other information, such as the date you made it and the number of the draft. Look at the file name below.

> RJan0395.002

This name tells you right away that:

1. The file contains your résumé: **'R'** (for résumé).
2. The résumé was prepared on January 3, 1995: **'Jan0395'**.
3. This is the second draft of the January 3, 1995 résumé: **'.002'**.

☐ **8. *Save your draft on a labeled disk* 💾. *Back it up on another disk*.** Reserve one disk for your résumé and personal statement. Prepare a back-up copy of that disk in case the first disk "crashes." *Label* the disks with your name, disk contents, institution, and your telephone numbers (see below) so they can be returned to you if you lose them. Store the disks in separate locations. Make sure you have your latest version saved in the following two ways. First, save it in the word processing format you use (containing any special fonts of type and styles you used). Second, always save an additional version in an ASCII (print) file on each disk. The institution to which you go next may not have the same computer or word processing program that you originally used, and any program should be able to read your ASCII file.

> S. C. Martinez, PharmD
> Résumé Disk
> College of Pharmacy, University of Texas
> 512-555-6640

☐ **9. _Print your first draft on white paper using a laser or ink-jet printer._** Why use a laser or ink-jet printer for the draft versions? Very simply, it makes your life much easier. Using these printers makes the drafts easier to read (for both you and other reviewers). It also guarantees that the spacing and formatting on your final copy will be the same as on any draft version. Use white paper because it is relatively inexpensive and can be recycled.

> **_Suggestion:_** Label each printed draft version with its number and date on a "header" (i.e., something you can put at the top of each page. Look under "header" in your word processing program's documentation manual.) As can be seen below, such a header makes it easy to keep track of revisions.

Draft 002 / January 3, 1995

The header above clearly shows that this is the second (002) version of the résumé prepared on January 3, 1995. Be sure _to remove this header before you print the final version_ of your résumé.

☐ **10. _Review/revise the first draft yourself._** Don't show the first draft to anyone. _You_ should review this draft for accuracy and completeness, and for proper grammar and spelling. (See Figure 4.1 for the first draft of a résumé with comments and corrections.) Mark any necessary corrections or changes in green or purple ink. (Avoid the trauma of red marks–they might bring back bad memories of your senior English class.) As you review the first draft, ask yourself if it honestly portrays your experiences. As mentioned previously, don't "pad" your résumé just to make it longer. Make all required changes using your computer, then save it to the hard disk and to a floppy disk. Be sure to revise the file name to reflect the new draft number. For example, label the fourth draft created on January 3, 1995 as RJan0395.004. Keep the old RJan0395.003 version on the disk–just in case something happens to the new RJan0395.004 file.

☐ **11. _Print your revised résumé on white paper using a laser or ink-jet printer._** This is the first draft you will show to others. Be sure that you check it for grammatical and spelling errors. Computerized "spell-checkers" are great, but be careful: _You no, of coarse, that they con miss sum spell errors._

☐ **12. _Get objective feedback from at least two people._** Look for honest reviewers who can proofread your résumé. Select critical reviewers who will do more than just scan the document and tell you that it looks fine.

One reviewer should be a _professional_ in the area to which you are applying. If you are applying for pharmacy school or a position as a pharmacist, ask a pharmacist to review your résumé. If you are applying for a family practice residency, ask a family practice faculty member to review your résumé. This "peer-professional" should identify potentially harmful or embarrassing technical

Figure 4.1: First Draft of a Résumé with Corrections

Avoid Courier type - try a font like Times Roman!

Include your first name →

Curriculum Vitae — *Delete — unnecessary*

D. P. Andrews
6784 East Broadway
Greenville, North Carolina 27857 *Add Telephone Number*

Delete this Section — not relevant

Personal Information
Social Security Number: 334-44-5678
Date of Birth: March 20, 1967
Marital Status: Married 3 yr to Mary
Children: 2 children (Mike & Kathy)
Health: Excellent

Eduction ← *Spelling error*

Delete high school information

East Rowan High School, June, 1986
Salisbury, North Carolina

Place in italics →

② N.C. State University,
Raleigh, NC
Major: Zoology, ~~August 1986~~ May 1990 *Just put year of graduation*
Graduated **summa cum laude**

Put the medical school info first in this section

① School of Medicine
East Carolina University, **May** 1994 *Delete the month if you have graduated*
Greenville, North Carolina
Doctor of Medicine

Honors and Awards

What was the award?

✱List med school honors first,
John P. Smith Award, 1989
Top Chemistry Major, N.C. State
University, 1990
undergrad second
Mary Smith Scholarship, 1986-1990 *What was this scholarship?*
Honors earned in Biochemistry, and ← *list clinical courses first*
spelling error → **Internl** Medicine
Phi Beta Kappa, 1990 *list first among undergrad honors - Accent this!*

Extracurricular Activities

List med school activities first in this category
Orientation Week **Counsilor**, 1987 *spelling error*
Wolfpack Athletic Booster Club ← *date?*
Pre-Med Club, 1989
Research with Dr. Wilson in ← *This fits better*
Biochemistry Department, 1991 *under a "Research Experience" category. Include the project title, university info, and dates*

Figure 4.1: cont'd

The interest is too broad. Specify it, such as "management of patients with MIs".

<u>Clinical Interests</u>
The human cardiovascular system

<u>Volunteer Activities</u> — *Too vague — list duties*
Hospital Volunteer, Rowan County
Hospital, Salisbury, N.C., 1983-84
Emergency Department, Central — *what did you do?*
Capitalize — Carolina Medical Center, 1986-1987
Service to the Underserved Medical
Student Group, 1990-1982

<u>Employment Experience</u> — *Delete this entry, especially if space is a problem.*
Cashier, Bill's Diner,
Salisbury, N.C., 1983
Clarify by briefly listing duties → Emergency Department, Central
Carolina Medical Center, 1987-90

<u>Professional Organizations</u>
American Medical Association, 1990-
Present
American Medical Student Association,
1990-Present

<u>Personal Interests</u>
Describe what you like to read. → Reading, Anti-Authority Study Group
References — *Delete this if you do not want to limit your consideration for a position.*
Available upon request

Delete this. Of course you will supply them if someone requests. Prepare a list of references, but don't submit them until you are asked. Don't include relatives, friends, or general acquaintances. Include only those people who can attest to your Knowledge, skills, and abilities. For each reference, list the person's name, position, Company/institution, address, and Telephone number.

or profession-specific errors (e.g., position titles, clubs, or honor societies) that someone unfamiliar with that profession might overlook.

The second reviewer should *know you personally* and does not need to be a medical professional. This reviewer should ensure that the résumé accurately depicts you and your experiences. Ask this reader to tell you what stands out about your résumé. If you and this person disagree about which key points stand out, discuss and resolve the differences.

> **Caution:** Don't ask anyone to give you feedback about your résumé unless you are willing to listen. If you just want somebody to tell you that your résumé looks great, tell the readers that in advance. Especially in the case of academic advisors, also tell them (diplomatically) that you want to hear all their comments, but you reserve the right to make decisions about any changes. After all, it is *your* résumé.

Compare the reviewers' remarks. Where do they agree? Where do they disagree? What changes do they suggest? Make whatever changes you think will improve your résumé. If two or more reviewers suggest the same or similar changes, you should have a *very* good reason for not making that change. If you obtain drastically different comments from two reviewers, evaluate what you hear and, if necessary, ask a third person for feedback.

❏ **13. *Revise drafts as needed.*** It's perfectly normal to have three or more drafts before you are ready to print the final copy of your résumé. Don't rush the process.

❏ **14. *Compare your résumé with the "Résumé DOs and DON'Ts" in Chapter 3.*** Check your résumé to ensure it contains your name, current address, and telephone number(s). Also scan it for personal information that should be omitted (e.g., age, children's names, marital status). Also check it against Chapter 3's list of things to omit.

❏ **15. *Make one final draft.*** Check it one last time for grammar, spelling, and content accuracy.

❏ **16. *Print the final, polished copy of your résumé on good paper using a laser or ink-jet printer.*** Be sure to use quality paper. Refer to Chapter 3 for details on paper selection. Check to be sure you have removed the header identifying the version number, as well as the date. (Don't put a date on your résumé.)

❏ **17. *Check it again.*** Just to be sure, check the grammar and spelling one last time. If it is more than one page, staple the pages, since staples survive the mail better than paper clips. After these final checks, you are ready to . . .

☐ **18. *Mail it!*** Don't bend or fold your résumé. Mail it in a large envelope. An unfolded résumé is easier for people to photocopy and provides a better and more readable copy.

Good luck!

Congratulations! You have finished your résumé. You can mail it with pride. It looks polished, like a fine marble statue. Remember to update it every six months. I hope you get into the program or job you want! Drop me a line and let me know. Best wishes.

5: Health Professionals' Résumés: Examples

Reviewing sample résumés will give you ideas on how to design yours.

Actual résumés

This chapter contains examples of actual résumés. They show you how different people inventoried their personal experiences and, in their own ways, distilled and organized them onto paper.

The writers are real people (although the names and identifying information have been changed). I helped many of them develop their résumés. The résumés directly describe each person's personal and professional experiences–in their own distinctive ways. Many of them initially worried that they lacked enough experiences to have eye-catching résumés.

As you read these résumés, note the similarities and differences among them. What do you like about each résumé? What stands out in your mind after reading it? What experiences or skills do you share with each author?

Visualize the writer as you read each résumé. The résumés are printed as they were mailed. You see what the selection committee, program director, or employer saw.

I know you will enjoy these résumés as much as I do. I can picture the writer as I read a résumé. I deeply appreciate the writers' allowing me to share their résumés with you.

List of sample résumés

Name	Position applying for
1. Brenda Gonzales	Medical school
2. Jason C. Gerber	Medical school
3. Nicholas A. Nekrasov	Anesthesia residency
4. Annita C. Berkley	Family Medicine residency
5. Doris M. Schmidt	Family Medicine residency
6. Nicole C. Edwards	Family Practice residency
7. William T. Thompson	General Surgery residency
8. Paul R. Zimmerman	Neurology residency
9. Carole T. Pastorelli	OB/GYN residency
10. Vincent M. De Cecco	Osteopath-for residency
11. Alice C. Meyers	Pediatric residency
12. Jackson H. Taylor	Pediatric residency
13. Stanley T. Livingstone	Physician (IMG)-for residency
14. Charlene Wigford	Dental Hygienist
15. Yeh-Shan Hsu	Dentist
16. Sally K. Wright	Medical Technologist-Supervisor
17. Jane Smith	Nursing School-Faculty
18. Linda J. Hale	Registered Nurse
19. Claire E. Weintraub	Registered Nurse
20. Roy S. Fernandez	Paramedic
21. George W. Shaw	Pastoral Care
22. Harry D. Boeson	Pharmacist
23. Linda C. Waterman	Pharmacist
24. Marjorie Morningstar	Physical Therapist
25. James T. Dean	Physician-First job after residency
26. M.Y. Shah	Physician (FMG)-for job
27. Sylvia Ann Guthrie	Physician Assistant
28. Don Schula	Radiology Technician
29. Amy Beth Anderson	Rehabilitation Clinic Manager
30. Paul Shafer	Respiratory Therapist

Brenda Gonzales
1180 Euclid Avenue, Apt #34
Cleveland, Ohio 44108
(216) 555-8970

EDUCATION	**M.S.**	**Case Western Reserve University, 1993** **Cleveland, OH** **Major: Biology**
	B.S.	**Wake Forest University, 1991** **Winston-Salem, NC** **Major: Psychology** ***Cum Laude Graduate***

RESEARCH EXPERIENCE   Effects of Ethanol on Renal Microcirculation, with S.M. Symthe, Ph.D., Dept. of Biochemistry, Case Western Reserve University, 1992-93

Child Anxiety Inventory Project: Developed Questionnaire for Evaluation of Childhood Anxiety, with P.C. Bell, Ph.D., Psychology Dept., Wake Forest University, 1990-91

HONORS & AWARDS   Wake Forest University
Phi Beta Kappa
Barton Scholarship for Psychology major

EMPLOYMENT & TEACHING EXPERIENCE   Counselor, Cleveland Women's Shelter, 1993-94
Research Technician, Dept. of Biochemistry, Case Western Reserve University, 1992-93

LANGUAGE SKILLS   French (fluent)
Spanish (basic conversation)

EXTRA-CURRICULAR ACTIVITIES   DAK Sorority Member, 1987-91, active alumna
Hiking, Biking, Squash, Travel, Theater

Jason C. Gerber
3344 W. Scenic Way
Charlottesville, Virginia 22903
(804) 555-6789

EDUCATION	**B.S. in Biochemistry**	**1994**
	The University of Virginia, Charlottesville, Virginia	
	Magna Cum Laude Graduate	

**HONORS
&
AWARDS**

Highest Academic Distinction, 1993-94
Rombach Interfaith Interdisciplinary Scholarship
    Spring 1993
General Academic Scholarship, 1990-94
4th Runner-Up, University of Virginia Freshman
    Essay Competition, essay published in *A Student's*
    Guide to Freshman Composition, 1990
Phi Eta Sigma Freshman Honor Society

EMPLOYMENT

Biochemistry Teaching Assistant
    University of Virginia
    December 1992-May 1994

**EXTRA-
CURRICULAR
ACTIVITIES**

Charlottesville Homeless Shelter, 1991-94
    Volunteer Services Coordinator
Interfaith Ministries, 1989-93
    Missions Coordinator, 1991-92
Summer Exchange Program, Bolivia, 1992

LANGUAGE   Able to provide basic medical care in Spanish

AFFILIATIONS

S.I.M. International
St. John's Church, Charlottesville, VA

INTERESTS   Tennis, hiking, camping, fishing, reading

Nicholas A. Nekrasov

3344 E. Jones St.   Atlanta, Georgia 30319
(404) 555-4456   (404) 555-4455 Fax

Education

M.D.   Emory University School of Medicine, 1994
          Atlanta, GA

Ph.D.   Georgia Tech University, 1994
          Atlanta, GA
          Major: Electrical and Computer Engineering
          Minor: Physiology

M.S.E.E. University of Pennsylvania, School of Engineering and
          Computer Science, Philadelphia, PA, 1988
          Major: Bioengineering
          Minor: Electrical Engineering

B.S.E.,   University of North Carolina, Chapel Hill, NC, 1985
          Major: Bioengineering
          Minor: Electrical Engineering

Honors and Awards

Honors earned in: Anesthesiology, Obstetrics/ Gynecology,
     Psychiatry, Radiology, Pediatrics, Physiology, Pharmacology
Athens Friends of Emory Young Investigator Award, 1993
2nd Place, Medical Student Research Competition, 1992
Who's Who in the East, 1992, 1993, 1994
Who's Who in the USA, 1994
GTE Engineering Scholarship, 1988
Mildred P. Coitner Academic Scholarship, 1982-85

Grants and Fellowships

Alpha Omega Alpha Honor Society Research Fellowship, 1992-93
American Heart Association Fellowship, 1992-93
American College of Cardiology Research Grant, 1992
Emory University Medical Student Research Fellowship, 1991, 1992

Extracurricular Activities

Anesthesia Student Club, 1991--present
Co-Founder and President, M.D./Ph.D. Club, 1992-94
Member, Dean's M.D./Ph.D. Committee, 1993-94
Etta Kappa Nu, Electrical Engineering Honor Society, Georgia Tech
     University Chapter, Founding Member, 1988-94

Nicholas A. Nekrasov   2

Publications/Dissertation

Nekrasov N, Stout C: Power losses in the energy delivery system during ablation. *Blood* 1993;3:276-281

Nekrasov N: A thermodynamic model of radiofrequency catheter ablation for the treatment of cardiac arrhythmias, Ph.D. Dissertation, Georgia Tech University, Department of Electrical and Computer Engineering, 1994

Nekrasov N, Smith JC: Maximum myocardial lesion depth using radiofrequency energy delivered with a platinum electrode (submitted for publication)

Languages

Computer Languages: C, Pascal, Assembly, FORTRAN, BASIC

Professional Organizations

American Medical Student Association, American Medical Association, Georgia Medical Association, Institute of Electrical and Electronic Engineers, Bioengineering Society

Employment and Research Experiences

Principal Investigator - University Medical Center - Dept. of Internal Medicine, Section of Cardiology, Atlanta, GA, 1988-Present
Direct several projects using radiofrequency catheter ablation to treat cardiac arrhythmia. These include determining optimal delivery parameters for delivery of radiofrequency energy, computer modeling of ablation energy and its effect on the myocardium, characterizing energy losses in delivery systems, and determining temperatures within myocardium during ablation. Write protocols, obtain grants, manage budget, coordinate purchasing, coordinate and supervise multiple studies, supervise engineers and medical students, conduct experiments, analyze and prepare data for publication and presentation at national conferences.

Personal Interests

Swimming, running, cycling, restoring classic automobiles, designing audio equipment, cooking, snow skiing

Annita C. Berkley

5590 East Lansing Ave.
Salt Lake City, UT 84184
801-555-8856 (H)

Education

**1995
(anticipated)**

Doctor of Medicine
University of Texas Southwestern Medical School at Dallas
Dallas, TX

1991

Bachelor of Arts, Political Science Major
Vassar College
Poughkeepsie, NY

Awards received

Medical School:
> Honors earned in: Family & Community Medicine, General Surgery

Undergraduate School:
> Departmental Honors and Mark of Distinction awarded for Senior Thesis: "Effects of Politics on Women's Reproductive Rights."

Extracurricular activities

Medical Services to the Needy, Fort Worth, TX
> Prenatal Nutrition Project, Fall 1993-Spring 1994
> Navarro Neighborhood Clinic, Spring 1994

Assistance to the Disabled, Inc., Dallas, TX
> Participated in a class to examine the mythology of disability and to explore ways to improve quality of life and productivity, June 1994

Joann Jones Shelter for Battered Children and Women, Poughkeepsie, NY
> Provided emotional support and information to clients and acted as an advocate before the Department of Social Services, Family Court, and Criminal Court. Spring 1990-Summer 1991

Texas Women's Health Care Council

Speaker's Committee, National Conference on Women's Health Issues, August 1994

Language

Conversational and patient-care Spanish

Work experience

**January 1991 to August
1993**

Health Educator
Planned Parenthood
Poughkeepsie, NY
> Taught sexuality classes

Interests and activities

Biking, water skiing, and camping

Doris M. Schmidt

5546 Olympic Street
Seattle, Washington 98198
(206) 555-0984 (Home)
(206) 5553721 (Pager)

Education:	M.D.	University of Washington School of Medicine Seattle, Washington, (May 1995, anticipated)
	B.A.	Washington State University, 1991 Pullman, Washington Political Science

Honors: Family and Community Medicine

Language: Spanish, written & verbal

Specialized Experience:
Trauma Surgery Externship, 1995
Family Practice Rotation in Honduras, 1994
Intensive Spanish Program, Costa Rica, 1993

Teaching Experience:
Instructor, *Talks With Tykes*, 1992-present
Teacher and Program Planner, Medical Students
    Educating Teenagers (MEDSET), 1992-93
Instructor, Rural Aids Project, 1991-92

Research Experience:
Detecting Malnutrition in Children Under Ten,
    Mexico City, Mexico, 1994-95

Extracurricular Activities:
Medical School:
    Abused Children's Shelter Advisory Committee,
        1991-present
    Refugee Clinic, Caregiver and Co-founder,
        1991-present
    Christian Medical Society, 1992-present

Undergraduate School:
    AIDS Education Project, 1989-91
    Intercollegiate Volleyball, Fall 1988
    Intramural Volleyball, 1987-88

Professional Associations:
Washington Academy of Family Physicians, 1992-present
American Medical Women's Association, 1992-present
American Medical Student Association, 1991-present

Personal Interests:
Spending time with family and friends, reading, volleyball,
    outdoor recreation, travel.

Nicole C. Edwards
3334 E. 54th St.
Tucson, Arizona 85733
(602) 555-5567

EDUCATION:	University of Arizona College of Medicine	Tucson, AZ
1994	**Doctor of Medicine**	
	University of Arizona	Tucson, AZ
1990	**Master of Science** Pharmaceutical Sciences	
1986	**Bachelor of Science** Biology	
1986	**Bachelor of Arts** Oriental Studies	
	National Taiwan Normal University	Taipei, Taiwan
1987	Mandarin Training Center	

HONORS/ AWARDS:

Medical School
Honors earned in: Family Practice, Pediatrics Perinatal Medicine, Surgery, Coronary Care Unit, Urology

Graduate School
1989-90   Regents Academic Scholarship, College of Pharmacy

Undergraduate School
1985-86   Dean's List
1987   Exchange Student Scholarship, Dept. Of Oriental Studies

ACTIVITIES:

Medical School
1993   Co-Director, Arizona Family Practice Forum
Coordinated activities: organized first aid caregivers for the El Tour de Tucson cycling event and "Day with a Doc"; raised funds for scholarships and speakers

1991-94   Member, Student Council, College of Medicine
Speakers Committee, Residency Fair Planning Committee, Student Disability Insurance Committee

1992   Summer Externship, Arizona Area Health Education Center Extension Program, Pinetop, AZ

1991   Delegate, American Medical Student Association Conference Kansas City, MO

Graduate School
1988-90   Volunteer, Planned Parenthood

Undergraduate School
1985-86   Volunteer, Student Health Center
1982-86   Volunteer, American Red Cross

Nicole C. Edwards   2

RESEARCH:

1990   *The effect of aspirin on solubility of diazepam and phenytoin,*
            Masters Thesis

1990   *Reporting of allergic reactions by patients to their physician,* under
            H. Smith, Pharm.D.

1989-90   *Prediction of solubility of organic compounds in binary and ternary
            systems,* under C. Samuelson, Ph.D.

1989-90   *Designing drug delivery systems for terfenadine,* under
            C. Samuelson, Ph.D.

EMPLOYMENT: *University of Arizona*   *Tucson, AZ*

1988-89   Laboratory Assistant, Dept. of Pharmacy
1985-87   Laboratory Assistant, Dept. of Animal Science
1984-85   Clinical Assistant, Dept. of Family Practice

TEACHING:

1989-90   Tutor, Office Minority & Student Affairs, University of Arizona
1989   Math and science tutor for high school and college students
1987   English teacher, Taipei, Taiwan

LANGUAGES:

Fluent in Mandarin Chinese
Working knowledge of Spanish

INTERESTS:

Family, travel, Chinese cooking, reading, photography,
calligraphy, and walking

William T. Thompson
4456 North French Dr.
Ann Arbor, Michigan 48120
(313) 555-6754

---

degree:	**Doctor of Medicine**	**May 1995 (anticipated)**
	University of Michigan Medical School	
	Ann Arbor, Michigan	
	Bachelor of Arts in Economics	**1991**
	Northwestern University	
	Evanston, Illinois	

honors: *Medical School:*
Surgery, Surgery Sub-Internship, Surgical Anatomy Elective, Neurology,
  Psychiatry, Neurosciences, Biochemistry, Molecular and Cellular
  Biology, and Behavioral Sciences
Commendation for Outstanding Academic Performance, 1994
2nd place, Oral Presentation, Michigan Medical Student
  Research Forum, 1993
Eli Lilly Scholar, Department of Pharmacology, 1993
Medical Student Summer Research Fellowship, 1992

Undergraduate School:
Honors Program in Medical Education, 1989-91
Dean's List, Fall 1988-Spring 1991

activities: Curriculum Analysis and Planning Project, 1994
College of Medicine Residency Fair and Career Week, Co-organizer, 1994
Medical Student Council Treasurer, 1993-94
College of Medicine Budget Reduction Ad Hoc Committee, 1993

publications: Thompson WT, Jones C: Characterization of naltrindole binding to delta
  opioid receptors in rat brain, *Biology.* 33:PL-223 to PL-224, 1992
Thompson WT, Smith C: *Leiomyosarcoma: A literature review,* (in preparation)

abstracts and presentations: Thompson WT, Jones C: Characterization of specific tritiated naltrindole
  binding to delta opioid receptors in rat brain, *Science.* 33;1:1A, 1993
  Presented at the North Central Student Medical Research Forum, Ann
  Arbor, Michigan, 1993 and at the Michigan Medical Student Research
  Forum, Ann Arbor, Michigan, 1992
Smith C, Thompson WT: The stable expression of tachykinin peptide NK_2
  receptors in murine fibroblast B82 cells, *Biology.* 38;1, 1990

languages: Spanish: proficient in conversation and reading

interests: Basketball, racquetball, golf, weightlifting, deep-sea fishing, travel

Paul R. Zimmerman
444 S. Euclid
Pittsburgh, Pennsylvania 15263
(412) 555-4538

Education	M.D.	University of Pittsburgh, 1995 (anticipated) Pittsburgh, PA
	B.S.	Philadelphia College of Pharmacy and Science Philadelphia, PA Major: Pharmacy, 1987

Honors/Awards

Honors earned in Neurology and Surgery clerkships, and Neurology Practice elective
Graduated *cum laude*, B.S. Pharmacy

Extracurricular Activities

Homeless Shelter Outreach Program, Pittsburgh, PA, 1991-1993
Pennsylvania Army National Guard, 1981-1987

Clinical Interests

Neuroanatomy, Pathophysiology, Infectious Disease, Clinical Pharmacology, and Pathology

Employment Experiences

Hospital/Clinical Pharmacist
   Pharmacist Relief, Pittsburgh, PA, 1992-Present
   U.S. Public Health Service, Pittsburgh, PA, 1987-Present
   Sisters of Mercy Hospital (Pharmacy intern), Philadelphia, PA, 1984-1987
Surgical Technician
   Shady Side Medical Center, Philadelphia, PA, 1982-1984
Laboratory Technician
   Pennsylvania State Health Laboratory, Philadelphia, PA, 1979-1982
   Merichem Co., Houston, TX, 1975-1977

Licenses/Certifications

Registered Pharmacist, Pennsylvania
Basic Cardiac Life Support (expires 1996)

Professional Organizations

American Academy of Neurology
American Society of Hospital Pharmacists
Pennsylvania Pharmacy Association

Languages

German (intermediate)
Spanish (basic), written & conversational

Personal Interests

Hiking, Nordic skiing, fingerstyle guitar, gardening, geology, natural history

CAROLE T. PASTORELLI

3355 North East State Drive
Hanover, New Hampshire 03755
(603) 555-6767

EDUCATION

Dartmouth Medical School, Hanover, New Hampshire
Doctor of Medicine, 1995 (anticipated)

Dartmouth College, Hanover, New Hampshire
Completed medical education prerequisites, 1990-91

New York University, Jones School of Business
Graduate Division, Graduate School of Arts & Sciences
Graduate studies in International Business & Politics, 1988-90

New York University, Smith School of the Arts
B.F.A., Photography and Politics, 1988

HONORS AND AWARDS

Honors in: Obstetrics and Gynecology Subinternship,
Psychiatry Clerkship, Surgical Subspecialty Clerkship
Army Health Professions Scholarship Program, 1991-Present

ACTIVE DUTY TRAINING ASSIGNMENTS (ACDUTRA)

Obstetrics and Gynecology, Fort Sam Houston, San Antonio, TX, 1994
Internal Medicine, Wilford Hall Medical Center, San Antonio, TX, 1993

RESEARCH EXPERIENCE

"The effect of monoclonal antibodies on p-24-Antigenemia in mice" with
E. M. Michaels, M.D., Department of Internal Medicine, Dartmouth
Medical School, 1989

PROFESSIONAL CERTIFICATION

Pediatric Advanced Life Support, 1994

COMMUNITY ACTIVITIES

Peer Reviewer, *The Book: A Third-Year Survival Manual,* 1993
Coordinator, Dartmouth Medical School Career Week & Residency Fair
Planning Committee, 1993-94
President, New Hampshire Chapter, American Medical Student
Association, 1992-93
Co-Editor, Women in Medicine Newsletter, AMSA Task Force Quarterly,
1993-94
Battered Women Assistance Project, 1992-93
Dartmouth Medical School Minority Recruitment Project, 1991-Present

Vincent M. De Cecco, D.O.

885 Beltline Road
Miami, Florida 33112
(305) 555-1234 [Home]
(305) 555-3208, pager #999 [Office]

Objective

Comprehensive training in Family Medicine including appropriate procedures and Obstetrics applicable to urban or rural settings.

Education

D.O., Kirksville College of Osteopathic Medicine, 1994
Kirksville, Missouri

Pre-Medicine, University of Miami, 1986-1989
Miami, Florida

B.A., University of Northern Colorado, Psychology, 1978
Greeley, Colorado

Undergraduate Studies, University of the Americas, 1974
Cholula, Puebla, Mexico

Post-Graduate Medical Education

Intern, Miami General Hospital
Miami, Florida, June 1994-Present

Honors/Awards

Fellow, Department of Osteopathic Manipulative Medicine
Kirksville College of Osteopathic Medicine, 1994

Miami Osteopathic Medical Foundation Scholarship, 1993

Certifications

Advanced Cardiac Life Support

Professional Associations

American Academy of Osteopathy, 1992-Present
Christian Medical and Dental Society, 1991-Present
American College of General Practitioners, 1990-Present
American Osteopathic Association, 1990-Present

Employment Experience

Executive Director, Business Computer Systems
Miami, Florida, 1985-1989
Multiple positions: computer retail, free-lance writer,
and computer consultant, 1978-1985

Alice C. Myers

PRESENT ADDRESS:
8878 N. Scott, # 17
Tucson, AZ, 85748
(602) 555-0090
[until 6/94]

PERMANENT ADDRESS:
135 E. Indian Circle
Phoenix, AZ 85032
(602) 555-3476

Medical Education

M.D.,   University of Arizona College of Medicine, 1994

Honors

Pediatrics, Pediatric Critical Care, Internal Medicine, Psychiatry, Surgery

Activities

American Academy of Pediatrics
Arizona Pediatric Forum
     Marketing Chairman, 1993
     Scholarship Committee, 1993
Internat'l Health Medical Education Consortium, Student/Resident Action
     Group, Class Representative and National Coordinator, 1992-94
Founder, Unified Health Student Consortium

Research

Epstein-Barr Virus and Lymphoproliferative disorders in Post-Liver Transplant
Patients at St. Ann's Hospital for Sick Children. Principal Investigator:
Mary Jacobs, M.D., in progress

Other Education

B.A.,   University of Arizona College of Arts and Sciences, Dept. of Humanities
         Major - German; Minor - Biology/Chemistry/Physics, 1990

Honors

Dean's Academic Award; Dean's List
Golden Key National Honor Society
Outstanding College Students of America
Who's Who Among American Colleges and Universities
Recognized as one of the top ten seniors of Sigma Delta Tau National Sorority

Research

"Smoking and Diet Among Teenage Girls," Principal investigator: M. Smith,
     Ph.D., Analysis of dietary data and smoking habits, January-May 1990

Language/Skills/International Experiences

Surgical tour to 3 small towns with 5 surgeons (Orthopedic, General, Gynecological),
     Ecuador, February 1994
General Surgery in small regional hospital, Nogales, Sonora, Mexico, August 1993
German Language Institute, Berlin, Germany, May-July 1989
Spanish: reading, speaking at intermediate level
German: reading, speaking, writing at intermediate level
Basic Cardiac Life Support

Jackson H. Taylor

1234 N. California St.
Irvine, CA 92718
213-555-5783

Medical Education

M.D., June 1995 (anticipated)
California College of Medicine,
University of California/Irvine
Honors:
    UCI-CCM Medical Student Award, 1993
    Mackenna Foundation Medical Scholarship, 1993
    Outstanding Second-Year Black Medical Student, 1993
    Outstanding First-Year Black Medical Student, 1992
    Ruth L. Lermen Foundation Medical Scholarship, 1992, 1993
Organizations:
    Student National Medical Association (SNMA), 1991-present
        Director, Region 1, 1992-93
        President, 1991-93
    American Medical Association, 1991-present
    California Medical Association, 1991-present
    Phi Delta Epsilon Medical Fraternity, 1991-92

Education:

M.A., Psychology, 1988
California State University, Los Angeles, CA
School of Letters & Sciences

B.A., Psychology & Sociology, 1986
University of Pennsylvania, State College, PA

Experience:

Children's Service Worker, 1990-91
    Los Angeles Department of Children's Services, Los Angeles, CA
        Supervision of abused neglected children, court officer.

Resident Counselor, 1988-90
    Booth Memorial Salvation Army, Los Angeles, CA
        Supervised troubled youth in resident home. Supervised
        mentally disturbed youth. Facilitated communication, family
        relations, and creative expression groups. Performed
        administrative duties and trained aides.

Stanley T. Livingstone

2543 N. Pasadena Rd., # 4
Long Beach, CA 90836
213-555-8760

Education:

Fifth Pathway Program, 1990-92
University of California-Irvine, California College of Medicine, Irvine, CA

Diploma in Medicine and Surgery, 1990
Centro de Estudios Universitarios Xochicalco (CEUX), School of
Medicine, Ensenada, Baja California, Mexico
  Class rank: top 2%
  Co-chair, Student/Administration Liaison Council, 1988-90
  Peer Counselor, 1988-90
  Student-body president, 1987

Graduate studies in Biology and Chemistry, 1983-84
University of the Pacific (UOP), Stockton, CA
  Chapter Vice-President, Alpha Chi Sigma Fraternity, 1984

B.A., Environmental Studies with Honors, 1980
University of California-Santa Barbara, Santa Barbara, CA
  Member, University Student Rescue Service, 1978-80, effected
    inclusion in county-wide advance life support system, 1980
  Developed and guided University-Isla Vista Health Awareness
    Program, 1978-80
  Executive Producer, News & Special Events, KCSB-FM public
    radio, 1979-80

Certificate, Mobile Intensive Care Paramedic, 1981
  Daniel Freeman Paramedic School, Inglewood, CA

Research:

Protoporphoryn synthesis development project, Department of
  Chemistry, University of the Pacific, 1983-84

Professional Experience:

Senior Paramedic, Doctors Ambulance, Modesto CA, 1983-86
Chairman, Education Committee, CA Rescue Paramedic Assoc., 1983
Director, Pre-hospital care, Patterson Hospital District, Del Puerto
  Hospital, Patterson, CA, 1981-83. Established full-time hospital-
  based advanced life support service

Certifications:
ACLS, USMLE, ECFMG

Interests:
Medical Spanish, fluent
Racquetball, gourmet cooking, bicycling, travel

Charlene Wigford

100 W. 79th St.
New York, NY 10041
(212) 555-7654
messages taken

143 Main St.
Laramie, WY 82070
(307) 555-4534
after December 15, 1994

Objective

Employment as office manager and dental assistant for a dental office with the opportunity to produce and present patient-education programs.

Education

New York City Community College, Brooklyn, NY
Associate Degree, Dental Hygiene, 1989

Work Experience

Dental Assistant, D.B. Green, D.D.S., Brooklyn, NY, 1991-Present

Assist with minor surgery and routine dental procedures. Developed method to automatically mail check-up reminders to patients. Manage office appointments, patient records and payments. Explain post-operative instructions to patients.

Dental Assistant, Dr. Zee Munforth, D.D.S., Brooklyn, NY, 1989-1991

Assisted at chair in busy periodontic practice, sterilized instruments, took and processed x-rays, cleaned teeth, charted mouths, and performed routine fluoride treatments. Also prepared filling compounds and solutions as needed. I also worked in the office making appointments, filing records, and doing bookkeeping.

Special Experience

Office Practice Course offered by New York Society of Dental Hygienists

Assisted in public education seminars given by the New York Dental Society. Demonstrated proper flossing and oral hygiene to school children.

Activities

Dental Assistant, New York Free Clinic, 1988-89. Cleaned teeth and took x-rays. General office duties. Participated in sessions given at Free Clinic to educate public on dental hygiene.

Interests

Hiking, horseback riding, Native American art, theater

Yeh-Shan Hsu, D.D.S.

Channel Dental Center, Inc.
9873 Gulf View Drive   **Office**
Houston, Texas 77048
(713) 555-9874

8749 Malcolm Grove Drive   **Home**
Katy, Texas 77449
(713) 555-9987

Professional Experience

Dentist, Channel Dental Center, Houston, TX, 1982-Present
Founded and currently maintain private practice of general dentistry. Practice includes fixed and removable prosthodontics, oral surgery, pedodontics, periodontics, endodontics, and restorative dentistry.

Mechanical Engineer, Texaco, Inc., Houston, Texas, 1977-78
Maintained a satisfactory level of production oil in assigned field. Involved with drilling new wells and water-flood projects.

Dental Licensure
Texas, expires June 1998

Education

D.D.S.   University of Texas Health Science Center/San Antonio
San Antonio, TX, 1982

B.S.ME.   Baylor University, Waco, TX, 1977

Honors and Awards

Omicron Kappa Upsilon, National Honorary Dental Society
Pi Tau Sigma, National Honor Society for Mechanical Engineering Students

Professional Organizations

American Dental Association
Texas Dental Association
Methodist Medical-Dental Fellowship

Personal Interests
Deep-sea fishing, sailing, bicycling

Sally K. Wright
3211 South Main Avenue
Albuquerque, New Mexico 87135
(505) 555-3863 (Home)
(505) 555-4582 (Office)

Objective:

A challenging position as a Laboratory Supervisor with the opportunity for professional growth where I can use my abilities to their fullest.

Employment Experience:

Laboratory Supervisor/Medical Technologist, Albuquerque Internal Medicine, P.C., Albuquerque, New Mexico, 1991-Present
Perform specialized laboratory procedures to help physicians diagnose patients' conditions and monitor the effects of therapy. Conduct and evaluate the results of established quality control procedures on tests, equipment, reagents, media, or products; and implement corrective action when indicated. Operate, calibrate, and maintain laboratory equipment, including correction of basic instrument malfunctions. Responsible for ordering and inventory of supplies. Supervise and train other laboratory technicians.

Product Specialist, Medical Information Systems, Inc., El Paso, Texas, 1991-1992
Helped develop, test, and troubleshoot the Medical Laboratory Information System.

Medical Technologist, Microbiology, El Paso Regional Medical Center, El Paso, Texas, 1988-1991
Performed microbiological testing procedures to help physicians determine patients' diagnoses and to monitor the effects of therapy.

Laboratory Technician, University Medical Center, Albuquerque, New Mexico, 1986-1988
Processed patient information and specimens for microbiological and serological testing according to established procedures. Ordered laboratory tests through laboratory information system. Prepared media and reagents.

Education:

Certificate of Medical Technology, 1988
University of New Mexico, Albuquerque, New Mexico

Bachelor of Science, 1985
University of New Mexico, Albuquerque, New Mexico
Major: Microbiology
Minor: Chemistry

Professional Societies:

American Society of Medical Technology
American Society of Clinical Pathology
National certification through Registry examination

Jane Smith, R.N., FNP, MPH

6884 East Northern Lights Circle   218-555-5656 (Office)
Duluth, Minnesota 55819   218-555-6868 (Home)

EDUCATION

University of Minnesota School of Medicine Duluth, Minnesota	Fellowship in Faculty Development 1993-1994
San Diego State University San Diego, California	Masters in Public Health, 1988-1989 Maternal and Child Health
Eastern Illinois University Charleston, Illinois	Bachelor of Arts, 1981-1983
University of Arizona College of Nursing Tucson, Arizona	Certification, 1976-1977 Family Nurse Practitioner
Parkland College Champaign, Illinois	Associate Degree in Nursing 1972-1974
University of Illinois Champaign, Illinois	Psychology/Sociology 1967-1970

MAJOR FIELD AND LICENSURE/CERTIFICATIONS

Major Fields: Family Medicine, Primary Care, Adolescence & Maternal & Child Health

Licensure/Certifications: Minnesota:
    Registered Nurse (R.N.)
    Family Nurse Practitioner Certification
U.S. Drug Enforcement Administration:
    Controlled Substance Registration
    Certification Schedules 2, 2N, 3, 3N, 4, 5

EMPLOYMENT

Family Nurse Practitioner, Clinical Lecturer, July 1989-Present
Department of Family and Community Medicine
University of Minnesota School of Medicine, Duluth, MN

Provide urgent and primary care in a Family Medicine residency training program. Conducted an audit of children with failure to thrive and developed a protocol, flow sheets, and tickler system for tracking these children. Developed a computer-based case management system for tracking "at-risk" prenatal and pediatric patients, and children with failure to thrive. Certified as Master Instructor in the Denver II.

Jane Smith, R.N.   2

Family Nurse Practitioner, Coordinator, April 1985-March 1988
Teen Clinic, Pecos Valley Medical Center, Pecos, NM

Provided primary care in this rural mountain community-based clinic as a National Health Service Corps solo provider. Developed a school-based clinic at Pecos High School which provided primary health care, family planning counseling, and mental health and substance abuse counseling to 300 junior and senior high school students.

Family Nurse Practitioner/Administrator/School Nurse, Oct 1978-Feb 1985
Multi-Service Center/Carolina Montoya Clinic, Santa Fe, NM

Provided primary care, administered, and directed this rural community-based clinic. I was a career Civil Service, National Health Service Corps (NHSC) solo provider until 1983 when an NHSC physician joined the clinic. Served as school nurse for local schools, taught health education classes, gave sports physicals, assessed students for learning disabilities, and provided first aid at sports events. Co-taught Emergency Medical Technician classes and helped EMT's develop a First Responders group. I taught prenatal classes and helped the Town of Santa Fe write a community block grant for the building of a new clinic.

Nurse Practitioner, Assistant Medical Director, July 1977-March 1978
Family Planning Center, Albuquerque, NM

Provided family planning, treated sexually transmitted diseases, and gave prenatal care at two clinics near Albuquerque. Taught in-service education classes to staff and family planning education in high schools.

Nurse Practitioner Student Preceptorship, January 1977-June 1977
George Spikes, M.D., Douglas Clinic, Douglas, AZ

Assistant Charge Nurse, September 1975-September 1976
SICU, St. Mary's Hospital and Health Center, Tucson, AZ

Staff Nurse, September 1974-August 1975
SICU, Tucson Medical Center, Tucson, AZ

Nursing Assistant/Student Nurse, October 1972-June 1974
Surgical ward and SICU, Carle Foundation Hospital, Urbana, IL

PRESENTATIONS TO MEDICAL STUDENTS AND RESIDENTS

Adolescent Health and the "HEADS(S)" Assessment
Learning Disability Assessment
Parenting Assessment in Primary Care
Adolescent Pregnancy
Outpatient Management of Children with Failure to Thrive
School Health and the Role of the Family Doctor
Development Assessment: The Denver II
The Role of the Mid-level Provider
A Public Health Perspective of Maternal and Child Health

Jane Smith, R.N.   3

ACADEMIC APPOINTMENTS

Clinical Lecturer, Department of Family and Community Medicine, 1989-Present
University of Minnesota School of Medicine, Duluth, MN

Clinical Lecturer, School of Public Health, 1993-Present
University of Minnesota School of Medicine, Duluth, MN

HONORS AND AWARDS

Small Clinic of the Year Award, for the Pecos Teen Clinic, New Mexico Primary
Care Association, 1987
Certificate of Appreciation, National Health Service Corps, Region IX, 1982

COMMITTEES

Mayor's Committee for Children Friendly Duluth, Child Health Committee, 1993
Schools as Family Resource Centers, 1993
Institute of Medicine, Department of Health Services, Washington, D.C., Committee on Primary
Care, July 1991
Northeast Unified School District
Adolescent Health Advisory Committee, April 1991-Present
Health Curriculum Advisory Committee, 1990
Maternal and Child Health, School of Public Health, San Diego State University
Student/Faculty Advisory Board, 1988-89
New Mexico Primary Care Association, Providers Advisory Board, 1985-88
Southern New Mexico Area Health Education Center, Advisory Board, 1984-85
Santa Fe Emergency Medical Service Coordinating Council
Founding Member, 1981-85
New Mexico Association Community Health Centers
Executive Board of Directors, 1980-85

PROFESSIONAL SOCIETIES

American Nurses Association
Minnesota Nurses Association
Board of Directors, 1992-94
American Public Health Association
Minnesota Public Health Association
Vice Chair, Medical Care Section, 1993-Present

MEDIA

"Back Country Doctor," Copperstate Cavalcade, KDUL-TV, Duluth, MN, 1983

Jane Smith, R.N. 4

SCHOLARLY PRESENTATIONS

Denver II, Developmental Assessment in Primary Care, Primary Care Update, University of Minnesota School of Medicine, Duluth, MN, March 1994

Outpatient Management of Children with Failure To Thrive, Primary Care Update, University of Minnesota School of Medicine, Duluth, MN, April 1993

School-based Health Care, Primary Care for Children, Minnesota Public Health Association St. Paul, MN, October 1991

School-based Health Care, Minnesota State School Nurses, Minneapolis, MN, August 1991

School-based Health Care, Poster Session, Northern Research Conference, University of Minnesota, Duluth, MN, April 1991

Rural Providers: The Role of the Nurse Practitioner, Rural Health Conference, University of Minnesota, Duluth, MN, 1990

Maternal and Child Health From A Public Health Perspective, Extracurricular class for first-year medical students, University of Minnesota School of Medicine, April/May 1990

Premenstrual Syndrome, Holy Cross Hospital, Jamestown, MN, 1983

Rural Providers, Panel Discussion, National Health Service Corps, Region XI, San Francisco, CA, 1982-83

GRANTS AND CONTRACTS

New Mexico Department of Health Services, Primary Care Grant (Awarded $7,000), Pecos Teen Clinic, Pecos, NM, 1986-87

Contract with Santa Fe County Health Department for Family Planning Services, by Santa Fe Multi-Service Center, 1982-85

Federal Jobs Bill Grant (Awarded $300,000), in collaboration with the Town of Santa Fe, NM To build a new clinic for the Santa Fe Multi-Service Center, 1983-84

Linda J. Hale, R.N.
3345 W. McHale Drive
New Orleans, Louisiana 70151
(504) 555-7878

Education:	Bachelor of Science: Nursing	1990
	University of Southwestern Louisiana	
	Summa Cum Laude	

Professional Experience :	Program Coordinator: Surgical Clerkship	1993 to present
	Dept. of Surgery, Tulane University School of Medicine	New Orleans, LA
	Administration, teaching, public relations, research	
	R.N.	1992-93
	Surgical Intensive Care Unit, VAMC	New Orleans, LA
	Preceptor: Oriented new staff members to the SICU. Six week program which emphasized technical skills, troubleshooting, problem solving, and ICU protocols	
	R.N.	1990-92
	Surgical Ward Charge Nurse, VAMC	New Orleans, LA

Licensure/ Certifications:	Registered Nurse, Louisiana State Board of Nursing	
	Critical Care Certification, New Orleans VAMC	
	Advanced Cardiac Life Support	
	EKG Interpretation Certification	
	Intra-Aortic Balloon Pump Certification	

Academic Honors:	Outstanding Senior Award, University of Southwestern Louisiana Foundation	1990
	Who's Who Among Students in American Universities & Colleges	1990
	Honors Program, College of Nursing	1988-90
	Coordinated Council of Student Nurses, Representative	1988-90
	Golden Key Honor Society	1988-90
	Academic Scholarship	1988-90

| **Professional Affiliations:** | Sigma Theta Tau | |
| | Association for Surgical Education | |

Professional Awards:	Excellence in Nursing Award	1994
	Presented by Veterans of Foreign Wars, VAMC	
	Outstanding Contribution to the Field of Surgical Education	1993
	Dept. of Surgery, Tulane University School of Medicine	

Linda J. Hale, R.N. 2

Publications:

Smith D, Hale LJ: Structured single-observer methods of evaluation for the assessment of ward performance on the surgical clerkship, *Surgery*. 1993;139:445-50

Ironbac C, Hale LJ: Test performance of a local exam at a non-local site for evaluation of surgical clerks, *Surgery*. 1994;140:233-35

Video Publications:

Hale LJ, Michael T: *Trust Me, I'm a Nurse: An exercise in interpersonal skills.* Video tape and instructional manual authorized for distribution by The Educational Clearinghouse, Association for Nursing Education, 1993

Grants:

Vernon Johnson Merit Review Grant ($4,000), Grant Proposal & Project Development: *The use of a self-paced radiographic teaching module designed to improve student interpretation of normal and abnormal findings on commonly ordered radiographic studies,* 1993

Presentations:

A model for the assessment of students' physician-patient interaction skills on the surgical clerkship. Presented at the National Association for Surgical Education Meeting, Portland, OR, April 1994

Assessing and improving students' physician-patient interaction skills: Intervention and follow-up. Presented at the National Association for Surgical Education Meeting, Dallas, TX, April 1993

Claire E. Weintraub, R.N.

856 East California Avenue
Palm Springs, CA 92234
(619) 555-9989 (Home)
(619) 555-5911 (Office)

Objective

A supervisory Registered Nurse position in a comprehensive cardiac rehabilitation center in the southwestern United States.

Employment Experience

Cardiac Rehabilitation Staff Nurse, January 1993-present
Palm Springs Medical Center, Palm Springs, CA
   Implemented patient cardiac rehabilitation plans with physicians and staff; instructed patients and relatives on exercise, diet, and other rehabilitation issues. Supervised unit nurses.
Assistant Coordinator of Cardiac Rehabilitation
   October 1993-March 1994

Cardiothoracic ICU Staff Nurse, January 1992-January 1993
Palm Springs Medical Center, Palm Springs, CA
   Monitored/provided nursing care to patients having heart or lung transplants, MIs, coronary-artery-bypass surgery, and cardiac-valve replacement/repair; coordinated care with physicians.

Newborn Nursery Staff Nurse, Yuma Regional Medical Center
   Yuma, AZ, May 1990-January 1993

EKG Technician, Yuma Regional Medical Center, Yuma, AZ
   April 1979- September 1980 and January 1988-May 1990

Specialized Training

Exercise Stress Testing with Nuclear Studies, Palm Springs
   Medical Center, Palm Springs, CA, 1994

Critical Care Nursing Internship Program, Palm Springs
   Medical Center, Palm Springs, CA, 1992

Education

Associate of Applied Science: Nursing, 1990
   Arizona Western College, Yuma, AZ
   Graduated with High Academic Distinction

Associate of Applied Science: Business & Fine Arts, 1986
   Arizona Western College, Yuma, AZ
   Graduated with High Academic Distinction

Licenses/ Certifications

Registered Nurse, California
Advanced Cardiac Life Support, expires June 1996

Roy S. Fernandez
4567 East College
Norman, Oklahoma 73019
(405) 555-9989

EDUCATION

University of Oklahoma, 1993-Present
Oklahoma City, OK
Major: Zoology

Norman High School, Diploma, 1988

EMPLOYMENT

Paramedic, St. Paul's Hospital and Medical Center
Norman, OK, 1994-Present

Emergency Medical Technician, St. Paul's Hospital and Medical
Center, Norman, OK, 1988-93

CERTIFICATIONS

National Paramedic Registry, 1994-Present
Advanced Cardiac Life Support Provider, 1994-Present
Basic Cardiac Life Support Instructor, 1990-Present
Emergency Medical Technician, Oklahoma, 1988-Present

TEACHING EXPERIENCE

Basic Cardiac Life Support

HONORS AND AWARDS

Undergraduate School
Dean's List

EXTRACURRICULAR ACTIVITIES

Student representative, Scholastic Conduct Committee, 1993-Present
High School AIDS Education Project, 1993-Present

PROFESSIONAL ORGANIZATIONS

National Association of Emergency Medical Technicians
1988-Present

OUTSIDE INTERESTS

Hiking, snow skiing, scuba diving

George W. Shaw, D.Min.

8900 East Lancaster Road, Farmington, Connecticut 06032
(203) 555-4376

EDUCATION

D.Min.	Golden Gate Theological Seminary; San Francisco, CA; 1991
Th.M.	Pastoral Psychology; Wake Forest University; Winston-Salem, NC; 1978
M.Div.	Virginia Theological Seminary; Richmond, VA; 1975
B.A.	Psychology; University of North Carolina; Chapel Hill, NC; 1972

CERTIFICATIONS

Supervisor, Association for Clinical Pastoral Education
Diplomate, American Association of Pastoral Counselors
Approved Supervisor, American Association for Marital and Family Therapy

CLINICAL TRAINING

ACPE Supervision and Pastoral Care
Bowman Gray Medical Center; Winston-Salem, NC
Eastern Virginia Medical School; Norfolk, VA

Pastoral Counseling
Bowman Gray Medical Center; Winston-Salem, NC
Virginia Institute of Pastoral Care; Richmond, VA
Pastoral Counseling and Consultation Centers of Philadelphia, PA
Philadelphia Family Guidance Clinic; Philadelphia, PA

Clinical Consultants
Richard Hodge, M.D.; Psychoanalytic Consultant; Houston, TX
Mary Webster, M.D.; Psychoanalytic Consultant; Philadelphia, PA
Alice Silverman, Ph.D.; Marriage and Family Therapy Consultant;
    Chicago, IL
James Simpson, Ph.D.; Structural Family Therapy Consultant;
    Chicago, IL
Judith Perry, M.D.; Marriage and Family Therapy Consultant;
    San Francisco, CA

PROFESSIONAL EXPERIENCE

Director-Pastoral Care and Education Department, 1990-Present
University Medical Center; Farmington, CT

Senior Staff and Faculty, 1985-1990
Lakeside Pastoral Counseling Center; Lutheran Medical Center; Chicago, IL
    CPE Supervising Consultant-Department of Pastoral Care
    Clinical Director-Lakeside Pastoral Counseling Center
    Supervising Faculty-Lakeside Hospital; Southport, IL
    AAMFT Supervisory Training Program in Marriage and Family Therapy

CPE Faculty and Supervisor, 1984-1985
Department of Pastoral Care and Education; M.D. Anderson Cancer
Center; Houston, TX

George W. Shaw, D.Min.   2

Director-Clinical Pastoral Education/Training Section, 1977-1984
Oklahoma Research Institute of Mental Sciences; Oklahoma Medical
Center; Oklahoma City, OK
    Adjunct Faculty-Graham Theological Seminary; Chicago, IL
    Adjunct Faculty-Institute of Applied Religion; New Orleans, LA
    Private Psychotherapy Practice

Coordinator-Clinical Pastoral Education Section, 1975-1977
    St. Joseph's Hospital and Medical Center; Richmond, VA

PROFESSIONAL COMMITTEES

American Association of Pastoral Counselors
    Eastern Regional Membership Committee
    Mid-West Regional Membership Committee

Association for Clinical Pastoral Education
    Eastern Regional Certification Committee
    Mid-West Regional Accreditation Committee

PROFESSIONAL PUBLICATIONS

"Integrating Religion and Counseling," *Pastoral Counseling Review,* February 1990, pp. 112-15

"The Pastoral Counselor's Role in a Medical Center Setting," *Journal of Pastoral Counseling*, March 1993, pp. 45-55

"Linking Patient Needs with Pastoral Counseling Services," *Pastoral Counseling Review*, June 1994, pp. 112-19

Harry D. Boeson
776 South Park Avenue   Columbia, South Carolina, 29259   (803) 555-5564

EDUCATION	University of South Carolina, Columbia, SC **Doctor of Pharmacy, 1994** University of South Carolina, Columbia, SC **Pre-pharmacy/Philosophy and Letters major, 1987-89**
RELEVANT EXPERIENCE	Pharmacy Intern, Philip's Rx, Columbia, SC, Jan 1993-June 1994 Assisted pharmacist with filling prescriptions, contacting physicians, and counseling patients regarding medication use. Operated cash register and computer systems. Intern/caseworker, Office of United States Senator Smith Columbia, SC, June 1993-Oct 1994 Liaison between constituents and the Senator. Responded to queries and dealt with federal governmental agencies to resolve constituents' problems. Informed Washington, D.C. office about local concerns. Emergency Medical Technician, Tarheel Ambulance Service Columbia, SC, Jan 1990-May 1993 Provided primary patient care and assessment in a prehospital setting. Maintained skills required on Advanced Life Support Unit as both a health care provider and an emergency driver. CPR Instructor, Medical Assistant, Receptionist, & Medical Records Clerk, University Medical Center, Columbia, SC, 1987-90 Assisted physicians, pharmacists, and nurses with primary patient care in a managed care setting. Taught CPR to students.
ACTIVITIES	CPR Instructor, American Heart Association, 1987-Present Teaching Assistant, Emergency Medical Technician Classes Columbia Community College, 1991 Volunteer, University Medical Center Emergency Department, 1987-89 Volunteer, St. Michael's Church Kitchen, Columbia, SC, 1987-89
HONORS	Knights of Pythias Scholarship, (Outstanding Pharm.D. Student), 1992 Vincentian Scholarship, (Outstanding Pre-Pharmacy Student), 1987-89 Valedictorian, St. Mary's High School, 1987 Varsity Letterman in basketball and soccer, 1984-87
PROFESSIONAL ORGANIZATIONS	American Pharmaceutical Association Academy of Students of Pharmacy Delegate for Region III, 1992-93 Chair of South Carolina Pharmacy Subcommittee, 1991-92 Kappa Psi Pharmaceutical Fraternity Chapter Vice-President, 1992-93 National Association of Retail Druggists American Society of Hospital Pharmacists North Carolina Pharmacy Association

Linda C. Waterman
3250 E. Washington Place
Hope, Arkansas 71801
(501) 555-7778

EDUCATION

Pharm. D., 1994
College of Pharmacy, University of Arkansas for Medical Sciences
Little Rock, AR

Pre-Pharmacy, 1989-91
Southern Arkansas University, El Dorado, AR

LICENSE Pharmacy Intern License, State of Arkansas

EMPLOYMENT EXPERIENCES **Pharmacy Intern,** University Medical Center, Little Rock, AR, 1992-94
Worked in decentralized inpatient and outpatient services. IV admixture compounding, repackaging supplies, and training technicians.

HONORS/ AWARDS Travel Award for Poster Presentation, Arkansas Society of Hospital Pharmacists 38th Meeting, Atlanta, GA, 1993
Charles M. Neilson Academic Scholarship, 1993
Tuition-waiver Orchestral Scholarship, Southern Arkansas University, 1989-91
Dean's List, Southern Arkansas University, 1989-91

PRESENTATIONS **Waterman LC,** Watson L: *Improving Student Participation at MCM and in Residencies.* Poster presentation at Arkansas Society of Hospital Pharmacists 38th Meeting, Atlanta, GA, 1993
Waterman LC, Jones WK: *Pharmacists Compliance With OBRA 90 at University Medical Center.* Poster presentation at Arkansas Society of Hospital Pharmacists 38th Meeting, Atlanta, GA, 1993

PROFESSIONAL ORGANIZATIONS Students of Arkansas Society of Hospital Pharmacists
Secretary/Treasurer, 1992-93
Coordinated programs for students to increase their participation at ASHP meetings and in residency programs. These included: poster presentations, local residency showcases, and workshops on interviewing and résumé-writing techniques.

LANGUAGES Spanish Immersion Program, Southern Arkansas University
Speak and write Spanish proficiently

VOLUNTEER/ PERSONAL INTERESTS University of Arkansas Student Health Center Pharmacy, 3 hours/week
October-December 1991
Travel, Orchestra, Worthy Inner Guard of Professional Pharmacy Fraternity

Marjorie Morningstar
3487 Peak Rd.
Albuquerque NM 87108
505-555-0870

Objective:

Working with children with developmental disabilities, both at school and at home.

Education:

University of Texas Medical Branch, Galveston, TX
B.S. in Physical Therapy, 1990
Graduated with High Honors

University of Texas, Austin, TX
September 1986-May 1988

Work:

Physical Therapist, 1993-Present
New Mexico Home Care Company, Albuquerque, NM
Work with elderly patients in home setting. Test range of motion, strength, and endurance. Assist in exercise and therapy routines. Coordinate home care treatment programs and monitor progress. Educate family care givers in proper technique. Prepare and adjust programs to fit the daily schedule of patients and their families. Keep records of treatment and progress of patients.

Physical Therapist, 1990-1993
Santa Fe School District, Santa Fe, NM
Worked with children ages birth to 21 years. Diagnosed sprains, strains, and ruptures. Took body fat, height, and weight measurements. Provided physical therapy when students needed it. Met with students' families and teachers to determine progress. Worked extensively with school-aged children with developmental disabilities. Devised games and exercise routines for children.

Organizations:

American Physical Therapy Association, 1988-present

Interests:

Volleyball, swimming, theater, skiing

James T. Dean

3345 E. Drake, Apt 22   Iowa City, Iowa 52242   (319) 555-3345

Post-graduate Education

1991-1994	Residency, Family Medicine, Michigan State University East Lansing, Michigan
1993-94	Chief Resident

Education

1987-1991	University of Iowa College of Medicine Iowa City, Iowa M.D.
1983-1987	Clarke College Dubuque, Iowa B.S., Zoology, *Magna Cum Laude*

Awards

1987	Dean's Scholarship, University of Iowa College of Medicine (one of five)
1987	Phi Kappa Phi, Clarke College
1987	Senior Honor Society, Vice President/Secretary

Research Experience

1992-93	Investigation of Pediatric Trauma in Rural Hospitals, under C. W. Buckmaster, M.D., Family Medicine, Michigan State University
1990	Medical Services for Children Project, under A. J. Hoyt, M.D., Family Medicine, University of Iowa College of Medicine

Licenses/Certificates

M.D., Michigan and Iowa
ACLS, expires 1996
ATLS, expires 1997

Extracurricular Activities

1991-1994	Residency Curriculum Committee, Member
1988-1991	Family Medicine Students Club, Member
1989-1990	Free Health Clinic, Worker
1989	Anatomy Course Evaluation, Curriculum Committee

Memberships

1991-Present	American Academy of Family Physicians

Outside Interests

Reading, aerobics, weightlifting, theater, sporting events, intramural athletics.

M.Y. Shah, M.D.
P.O. Box 1245
Laurel, MS 39438

601-555-4124 office
601-555-4782 home
601-555-8324 digital pager

EDUCATION:

M.B.B.S.: Medical College, Baroda, India, 1982

EXPERIENCE:

4/86-Present — Staff Physician, Dept. of Emergency Medicine, So. Mississippi State Hospital, Laurel, MS. Responsible for medical, pediatric, surgical, obstetric, orthopedic, and psychiatric emergencies. On-call every third day. Have been doing ACLS, BCLS, medical, and surgical procedures.

5/85 to 3/86 — Physician Assistant, Parlin Center for Women, Parlin, NJ (Ob/Gyn), and
Avenet Islin Medical Group, Avenet, NJ (Family Practice)

8/83 to 3/84 — Junior Lecturer in Physiology, Medical College, M.S. University Baroda, India

2/83 to 8/83 — House Physician, Emery Hospital (Salvation Army), Baroda, India

2/82 to 1/83 — Transitional Internship. M.S. University Affiliated Hospitals Baroda, India

RESEARCH: Epidemiological survey of pulmonary tuberculosis

MEDICAL LICENSE:

Mississippi

CERTIFICATIONS:

FLEX: Passed in California, June 1985

FMGEMS: Hold Standard ECFMG certificate

ACLS, ATLS, PALS: Hold current certificates

INTERESTS: Wildlife photography, soccer, hiking

Sylvia Ann Guthrie, P.A.

415 West 36th Street
Richmond, Virginia 23290
(804) 555-9112 (Home)
(804) 555-1288 (Office)

EDUCATION

Hahnemann Medical College, Philadelphia, PA, 1980
B.S., P.A., Physician Assistant Program

City University, New York, NY, 1974
B.A., Comparative Religion/Sociology

CURRENT MEDICAL LICENSURE

NCCPA
Physician Assistant, Virginia

EMPLOYMENT

Physician Assistant, Medical Associates Clinic, Inc., Richmond, VA, 1991-Present
Provide primary care for a multicultural patient population.

Physician Assistant, Richmond Psychiatric Institute, Richmond, VA, 1990-91
Evaluated patients upon admission to a drug and alcohol detoxification program.

Physician Assistant, Metro Health Plan, Richmond, VA, 1983-90
Provided primary care in a family practice outpatient setting. Managed patients five to sixty-five years of age, ranging from well-person visits to management of chronic illnesses.
Chair, Nurse Practitioner/Physician Assistant Dept. (from its inception), 1986-89
Member, Task Force on Parental Leave Policy, 1986
Member, Medical Council, 1985-88

Physician Assistant, Presbyterian-Univ. of Pennsylvania Medical Center, Philadelphia, PA, 1980-83
Treated patients in an Emergency and Walk-In Clinic in a large, urban hospital. Assessed and treated non-life-threatening problems in an ethnically/racially diverse community. Helped staff ENT Clinic during twice-weekly sessions.

Nutrition Education and Rural Health, U.S. Peace Corps, Philippines, 1975-77
Surveyed population to identify nutritional needs, planned and taught nutrition, health education, and family planning classes. Organized supplemental meal programs for preschoolers and pregnant women. Developed program to build water-seal toilets.

Sylvia Ann Guthrie, P.A.   2

OTHER HEALTH ACTIVITIES

Peace Corps Medical Contractor for 1991 CME/CEU Workshop with University of Virginia
International Health Program
Presented at two conferences in The Gambia and Zimbabwe.

Women's Delegation to Israel and Palestine, 1991
Interviewed Israelis and Palestinians about the effects of conflict on their mental and physical
health. Visited refugee camps, health care facilities, and community development projects.
Talked to human rights groups.

Virginia Task Force on Domestic Violence, 1990
Served on interdisciplinary, state-wide task force that recommended strategies to decrease
domestic violence.

PUBLICATIONS

Guthrie SA, Young AA: PA's teach health promotion in the Inner City, *AAPA Journal*, 12(4),
February 1992

PRESENTATIONS

Taking a sexuality history for primary care providers. Presented at Planned Parenthood Workshop,
Norfolk, VA, 1993

Abuse in adolescent dating relationships: Prevention in the health care setting. Presented at the
annual meeting of the American Public Health Association, New Orleans, LA, October 1991

COMMUNITY ACTIVITIES

Member, WSVA Community Advisory Board, 1988-91
Member, Women's Task Force on Women in the Workforce, 1989-90
Vice-President, Pleasant Valley Neighborhood Association, 1985-89

PROFESSIONAL ORGANIZATIONS

American Public Health Association
American Academy of Physician Assistants
Virginia State Association of Physician Assistants
Physicians for Human Rights
National Health Rights Network
National Women's Health Network

Don Schula

220 S. Second St.
Memphis, TN. 38104
(901) 555-1243

Objective:

Chief Radiology Technician

Employment:

Radiologic Technologist, 11/93-present
Methodist Hospital, Memphis, TN
Oversee operation of department. Schedule and train other technicians. Take and process radiographs. Troubleshoot equipment failures.

Radiologic Technologist, 1991-93
St. Francis' Hospital, Memphis, TN
Took and processed plain radiographs. Took call as "specials" and CT technician.

Radiologic Technologist, 1990-1991
St. Joseph's Hospital, Memphis, TN
Took and processed radiographs. Assisted other technicians and operated portable x-ray machine on wards and in clinic.

Education:

Shelby State Community College
Memphis, TN
Radiologic Technology, 1990
Summa Cum Laude

Interests:

Bowhunting, fly-fishing, Civil War battle recreations, kayaking

Amy Beth Anderson
22324 Barnhill Drive
Indianapolis, Indiana 46203
(317) 555-3122

Objective: *A position establishing, marketing, and managing a rehabilitation/wellness clinic in a medical center setting.*

Professional Experience

Assistant Manager   *1991-Present*
Medi-Fit Health & Fitness Center, Muncie, IN
> Supervis and train employees, market center services, coordinate computerized client billing, update business accounting records, analyze and interpret body composition via computer, and demonstrate proper use of fitness equipment to clients.

Specialized Rehabilitation and Wellness Training and Experience

Cardiac Rehabilitation Internship   *May-August 1994*
University Medical Center, Indianapolis, IN
> Coordinated cardiac rehabilitation activities with physicians and staff; adjusted exercise prescriptions, based on patient needs, for cardiac rehab in-/out-patients; evaluated patients' exercise tolerance using diagnostic telemetry, EKGs, blood pressure, heart rate, and subjective data; prepared patients for exercise treadmill testing (12-lead ECG).

Coordinator/Personal Training Practicum   *Spring 1994*
Ball State University, Muncie, IN
> Supervised undergraduate students during practicum.

Exercise Leader   *Fall 1993*
Ball State University, Muncie, IN
> Devised and led exercise routines in college aerobic class.

Personal Training Practicum   *Spring 1993*
Ball State University, Muncie, IN
> Assessed participants' fitness needs, planned personalized exercise programs, and educated participants about exercise and diet issues.

Salesperson   *Sept 1990-January 1991*
Michael's Department Store, Muncie, IN
> Sold fine jewelry, designed jewelry displays, recorded cash and credit card sales.

Education

Bachelor of Science   *1994*
Ball State University, Muncie, IN
> Major: Exercise Science and Wellness
> Honors: Shroyer Academic Scholarship
> Overall GPA: 3.45/4.0

Certification

Cardiopulmonary Resuscitation

Paul Schafer, R.T.

After October 1, 1994:   *Before October 1, 1994:*

37 Salem Ave, # 2B   135 Crestview Dr.
Boston, MA 02113   Framingham, MA 01701
617-555-1342   617-555-9876

Objective: Respiratory therapist at an urban teaching hospital.

Education:

California College for Respiratory Therapy, San Diego, CA
Diploma in Respiratory Therapy, 1991

Springfield Technical Community College, Springfield, MA
Emergency Medical Technician Program, 1989

Hampshire College, Amherst, MA
Bachelor of Arts in Music, 1989

Certifications:

Certified Respiratory Therapy Technician
National Board for Respiratory Care, 1991-present

Work Experience:

Respiratory Therapist, 1992-present
Framingham Hospital, Framingham, MA
Responsible for routine ventilator maintenance for all inpatients. On hospital's "Code Blue" team. Performed EKGs, pulmonary function exams, stress tests, and taught patient health education classes.

Respiratory Therapist, 1991-92
Southwest Community Hospital, San Diego, CA
Provided general respiratory therapy, including artificial ventilation, airway maintenance, ventilator installation, and "Code Blue" procedures.

Awards: Full scholarship, CA College for Respiratory Therapy, 1990-91
Deans List, Hampshire College, 1988-89
1st place: Trumpet, Wellington Jazz Competition, 1989

Interests: Trumpet, jazz, bowhunting, motorcycle racing and repair

6: What is a Personal Statement?

Tell others who you *really* are in your personal statement.

What is a personal statement?

A personal statement tells people, such as program directors, admissions officers and potential employers *who* you are. While résumés tell reviewers what you have done and how to locate you, personal statements describe the experiences and events that shaped your personality, values, and goals. You want to accurately transmit this information when writing your own personal statement.

Several years ago, a colleague referred Ted, a fourth-year medical student, to me. Ted was struggling with his personal statement. No wonder! The first thing Ted said to me was that he differed very little from all the other people who were applying for residency positions. He also stated that he was "average" academically. It was no surprise to me that, with this attitude, he had written a lackluster personal statement. It wasn't bad; it just failed to convey who Ted really was.

After chatting with Ted for about fifteen minutes, I compiled an inventory (discussed in Chapter 7) that included the following information. Ted

- grew up on an isolated farm.

- had eight siblings.

- performed daily chores in addition to excelling in his studies.

- delivered calves and cared for animals.

- was a devoted spouse and father with two young children.

Although I had never talked with Ted before, after just a few minutes I felt as though I had known him for years. The original personal statement Ted wrote didn't describe his rich experiences, values, independence, team spirit, and hands-on skills. An hour later, after Ted's brief self-evaluation and a little work using a word processor, he emerged from my office beaming with pride in his new personal statement that better revealed his true self.

Are you dissatisfied with the personal statement you wrote, or frustrated at the prospect of writing one? Join the crowd! It takes time, thought, and energy to write a good personal statement. It's easy to get "bogged-down" in the process–*unless you have a writing strategy.*

The next several chapters of this book will help you develop such a strategy, by providing an easy, step-by-step process to follow. Use it to write a personal statement that you may confidently and proudly mail to any admissions officer, selection committee, or potential employer.

Why write a personal statement?

Most health professions schools, residencies, fellowships, and employers require personal statements.

Your personal statement that helps readers better visualize you as an individual. It *describes* experiences that may or may not be included on your résumé and *explains* how you developed into the person you are today.

Selection committees and potential employers read applicants' personal statements to see if anyone stands out from the crowd. They consider a variety of factors when selecting applicants (K.V. Iserson's *Getting Into A Residency* provides a detailed description), and your personal statement must include information about you that is not found anywhere else in your application materials.

At any level, all applicants are "hard-working, disciplined, and dedicated to delivering excellent health care." This is boring! Stand out from the crowd by elaborating on your personal issues, life-changing experiences, family, goals, and expectations. Your personal statement will virtually jump out from the pile on the reviewer's desk when it discusses how your volunteer experiences influenced you to pursue a particular health-care field. Remember, *you are unique* and your personal statement must communicate that to the reader.

Personal statements are like Velcro™

Do you want your personal statement to "stick" to the readers' minds and make you stand out from your competition? Of course you do. Potential employers and people on selection committees review many application packets that contain similar résumés, test scores, and letters of recommendation. While they must evaluate these types of factual information, all of them fail to provide the vital "personal" connection. If you share a common interest with people, it's easier for you to "break the ice" and get to know them. Have you ever listened to a couple of scuba divers talking? What do they talk about? It's the same with pilots, computer hackers, paramedics, or dentists. Common interests are like the hooks on Velcro. They make a fast connection.

One physician interviewer told me that she reads *only* résumés and personal statements before interviews. She believes they give her a more accurate picture of the candidate. She recently encountered an applicant who wrote about an interest in vampire folklore. Since they shared this (admittedly uncommon) interest, they discussed the topic for the first ten minutes of the interview. The applicant felt more relaxed than during most interviews, was more open during the rest of that interview, and made a significant impression on the interviewer.

The Velcro strategy is simple

Reviewers seek applicants who will be happy and productive. They also often seek people similar to themselves. An applicant's experience as a ski instructor, Emergency Medical Technician, or computer hacker may mentally "link" him with interviewers looking for applicants who "fit" with their departments (and themselves).

> Ben, a fourth-year medical student applying for a hard-to-get position in orthopedic surgery, included a rich description of how collegiate hockey shaped his life in his personal statement. He doubted whether anyone either cared about or would relate to this part of his background. He was quite surprised when a residency program director, who had just read his personal statement, telephoned him one Sunday afternoon. The part about hockey "stuck" in this director's mind. Since the program's residents and attendings had a hockey team, they were interested in outstanding candidates who could also play hockey. Ben got the interview and, eventually, the residency position.

Note that Ben shared interests with this particular group, and he communicated this information via his personal statement. *Think* Velcro!

Conversely, you may reduce your chances of being interviewed for a position if your personal statement describes particular expectations or goals that institution cannot provide.

Jenny's personal statement described why she preferred to work in a fast-paced, urban setting. Yet she applied for several positions in the slower suburbs. Since her personal statement clearly discouraged these potential suburban employers, none interviewed her. She was actually very lucky, since she admitted that she would not have been happy working in a slow-paced setting.

Would you be happy in a position if you had to de-emphasize a very important element of your professional life?

In another case, Tanya told me that she definitely wanted to treat Spanish-speaking patients during her training, yet her personal statement did not mention this goal. When asked if she would be happy working at an institution that had few Spanish-speaking patients, she replied that she would not. I suggested that she (1) review positions with her advisor and apply only to those that matched her goal, and (2) specifically state her preference in her personal statement so she would not be disappointed.

Why do people struggle with personal statements?

Over the years, in working one-on-one with students who were struggling to write their personal statements, I have identified several reasons why people become so frustrated while writing these missives. Most individuals start by complaining that they are the only ones who find writing a personal statement hard. Not true! Most people have difficulty with the task. Understanding the *four roadblocks* to composing a personal statement is an important part of the writing process.

1. *Most people dislike writing positive things about themselves.* Even when they have accomplished a great deal, people hesitate to write statements that might be perceived as self-serving.

   Gail, a fourth-year medical student, was an accomplished researcher who had financed her education through research grants. Bob, a fourth-year dental student, had earned top grades in his "clinicals." Both students' personal statements initially downplayed their successes. Fortunately, they revised their personal statements to describe their accomplishments without inflating them. Gail stated that she wanted to conduct clinical research and was seeking a residency program that would prepare her to develop a research program of her own. Bob explained how his interest and skill in the mechanics of dental practice helped him achieve his fine grades and prepared him for an endodontics fellowship. Both students' accurate descriptions of their talents gave reviewers the information they needed to select them for their programs.

2. *Most people don't recognize their unique talents and traits.* Ted, the student-farmer described at the beginning of this chapter, clearly had a unique background. I sat enthralled as he talked about dividing chores with his siblings, delivering calves, and caring for sick and injured animals. In a short time I came to like Ted as a genuine human being who had won my trust. Ted also showed himself

to be a team-builder who could budget his time and perform complicated "hands-on" procedures. Completing a Personal Marketing Inventory (Chapter 7) allowed him to recognize his own talents and traits.

3. *People tend to compare themselves to others.* Who are you competing against? In reality, your competition for any position is an imaginary ideal who doesn't exist. By trying to compare yourself to others, you tend to focus on your shortcomings and overlook your strengths. This is the wrong approach. Use your personal statement to tell potential employers who you are, and, by focusing on your strengths, why you are best suited for the position you seek. Writing this kind of personal statement, however, requires a *marketing* strategy. Bob, Gail, and Sylvia (described below) initially asked "Why would anyone want me?" implicitly suggesting that selection committees would automatically pick other candidates. This is not true.

4. *Many people try to write their personal statements without a strategy.* All of us use strategies every day to accomplish complex tasks. For example, you probably have a grocery-buying strategy you use when you go to the store. If your goal is to buy, as cheaply as possible, only the items you need for a two-week period, how do you do it? What products do you select first? last? How do you travel through the store? Do you use a list? Though they may have strategies for relatively simple tasks such as buying groceries, many people attempt to write their personal statements without a similar plan. As a result, they sit and stare into space, waiting for divine inspiration that seldom comes.

> Sylvia, a biology major, was applying for medical school. In tears, she explained that she was frustrated after sitting in front of a computer for hours trying to write her personal statement. Sylvia had a lot of ideas, but she just couldn't get them on paper. Her tears, mumbling, and listening to advice from other students hadn't helped. Yet once Sylvia developed a writing strategy based on her personal strengths, she was able to write an excellent first draft of her personal statement within the hour.

There are, then, only two strategies you need–a *writing strategy* to produce a highly polished document, and a *marketing strategy* to include information potential employers want to see. The balance of this chapter and Chapters 7 and 8 discuss marketing strategies. Chapter 9 provides you with a writing strategy. The rest of the book puts it all together.

"Marketing" versus "selling" yourself

You are a product. In the business world, one would say that you are using the personal statement "to place" the product (you) in a favorable location (e.g., job, program, or school). To do this, you can try either to *sell* the product or to *market* it–your choice. What's the difference? Which method is more likely to succeed?

Selling

You have probably been approached by "pushy" salespeople who try to sell you products that you don't really want or need. These salespeople either provide little helpful information about the products, or inflate what they can do. They use "hard-sell" techniques to persuade you to buy the product. The same can be true for personal statements. Some students use these techniques to "play up to" selection committees.

Mike's personal statement included this sentence in his final paragraph: "I would really like to interview with your hospital." Ellen, a physical therapy applicant who had never volunteered to work with the indigent, wrote in her personal statement that she wanted to serve "needy people" after her training. Both of these individuals' personal statements used "hard-sell" techniques to try to convince the reviewers to choose them. These techniques rarely impress selection committees because they've seen plenty of them. Rather than using a "hard sell" to get an interview, *market* yourself to prospective employers.

Marketing

Use your personal statement to show selection committees that you are the best possible candidate for the position. Tell them what you have done and how you will enhance their departments. This is powerful.

Colleges, training programs, and employers know the value of marketing. They know what applicants seek and they design their marketing materials to show that they have it. Those materials were specifically designed to interest *you*, the prospective student, trainee, or employee in *their* institution. They invest much time and money in these materials to help you learn about them. They hope to attract applicants who will be productive and happy at their institutions. They know that happy and productive people usually stay in a position and promote the institution to future applicants. (Understand that while all programs and institutions have strengths and weaknesses, they rarely include a "weaknesses" section in their marketing literature.)

Use the same effective strategy to market *yourself* using your personal statement. It's easy to do. First, think of what employers, programs, and schools want in a candidate. Second, identify the qualifications you possess. Finally, match the two lists and use your personal statement to describe your qualifications that reviewers desire.

If this concept is still unclear, think of shopping for a computer. You first identify your needs: hard disk size, modem, floppy disk options, price limitations, etc. Then you acquaint yourself with the products that can meet those needs. You appreciate a salesperson who provides honest, straightforward product information that you can use to select a computer that is "right" for you. Reviewers work basically the same way. They want to select people who will succeed and thrive in a position. Give them the information they need to make their decisions.

One undergraduate student applying to a graduate program used this marketing strategy when she explained her research experience. Instead of merely describing her research project, she described the joys and frustrations of research and how participating in research developed her problem-solving, critical-thinking, and writing skills–all qualities she knew the selection committee sought in applicants. *Use your personal statement to market yourself.*

DEVELOPING YOUR MARKETING STRATEGY

Now, begin to develop your marketing strategy. First you will need to identify what qualifications selection committees desire from applicants at your level. Next, you must identify your strengths and then match your qualifications with those for the position you seek. These matches will provide the basis for your marketing strategy.

Reviewers look for specific attributes

Most selection committees seek common sets of qualifications, but each may emphasize some capabilities over others. Formally or informally, they probably use "Must/Want" analyses similar to those described for residency applicants by K. V. Iserson, M.D., in *Getting Into A Residency: A Guide For Medical Students* (see bibliography). A "Must" is a quality that an applicant *must* possess. For example, an institution that serves a diverse patient population would look for employees who easily work with people from differing backgrounds. Thus, *flexibility* and the *ability to accept others who are different* would be definite "Musts." A "Want" is a feature that is nice to see in an applicant, but the lack of which would not necessarily eliminate a candidate from consideration. The hiring team prioritizes these "Wants," giving some more weight than others.

In general, however, we know that most reviewers selecting among applicants for positions in the health professions look for evidence in the candidates of a good attitude, stability, interpersonal skills, academic performance, and maturity. As Dr. Iserson describes the system, the reviewers (often unconsciously) total the "scores" for each applicant, offering interviews and, ultimately, positions to those with the highest total on the reviewers' "Must/Want" scorecard.

While professional schools, programs or institutions tend to have similar selection factors, there can be differences. A program in the Southwest, for example, may prefer applicants who speak Spanish. In an area with few Spanish-speaking patients, other selection criteria will probably be emphasized.

In all cases, reviewers and selection committees try to optimize the match between their own goals, needs or the learning experiences they offer with the applicants' strengths and goals.

Now, identify what programs and potential employers are looking for. List the major strengths (e.g., skills, traits, experiences) *reviewers* want the person who fills the position to have. *This list may be different for every position, school, or program for which you are applying.* If so, you should make up a separate list for each: you will then need to customize your personal statement (and résumé) for each position. You can develop the list by talking to your peers, mentor/advisor, faculty, students, residents, and other professionals in the field. Also be sure to look in the published job description and review the program's and the institution's materials.

> Patti, about to graduate from a family practice residency, sought positions from three different groups. After reading the materials they sent her, she also checked with friends practicing in the areas where these groups were located. She discovered that one group looked for graduates with critical care experience, the second group desired to

hire those with considerable experience in Obstetrics, and the third wanted applicants who worked well with patients in long-term care facilities.

Ron, an undergraduate, could discern from published materials that two of the professional schools to which he wanted to apply stressed family and religious values. Another seemed to look for older students with "life experiences," and several others seemed to primarily desire women and minority students. He confirmed his impressions with the Dean of Students at each school.

Attributes your potential employers seek

In the spaces below, specify the attributes your potential employers or selection committees seek. This will help you to later are identify your own strengths to include in your personal statement. An example is provided.

Reviewers: "We want graduate students (employees) who can speak/learn Spanish."

Point 1: _____

Point 2: _____

Point 3: _____

Point 4: _____

Point 5: _____

Point 6: _____

Point 7: _____

Point 8: _____

Point 9: _____

Point 10: _____

Ready to write?

Not quite.

Before you begin writing, you have finish developing your marketing strategy. In Chapter 7 you will inventory your marketable traits and skills. Then, Chapter 8 will help you match these attributes with those that reviewers seek. By doing this you will finalize your marketing strategy. You will also learn how to describe your strengths in terms that reviewers understand. Finally, Chapter 9 provides a step-by-step writing strategy to produce your personal statement. Be sure to read the sample personal statements in Chapter 10.

Now, let's inventory your marketable attributes!

7: Your Personal Marketing Inventory: Identifying Skills and Traits

Inventory your strengths.

Show programs why they should want you

Many health professionals and students wander into my office and ask "Why would anyone want *me*?" They haven't thought about the qualities they possess that selection committees actively seek. They find it difficult to identify and describe their marketable strengths. As a result, they sell themselves short because they downplay or fail to specify some interesting and marketable personal attributes. You have to show reviewers why they should want *you*!

This chapter will help you define the marketable attributes you, yes, *you*, already possess. It contains a Personal Marketing Inventory that will help you *analyze* academic, extracurricular, and personal experiences, and *specify* your marketable skills and traits that reviewers seek. These are the "strengths" you will include in your personal statements when you apply for a professional school, residency program, fellowship, or other career positions. The Inventory takes 30 to 45 minutes to complete. It will be time well spent, because you may recall forgotten events or recognize skills that you have never thought about before.

Ted (farmer-student-family man first mentioned in Chapter 6) struggled to identify his marketable attributes. Yet during our interview, his strengths quickly emerged, and he easily incorporated them into his personal statement. The Personal Marketing Inventory contains the same questions I asked Ted–and would ask you if I were helping you write your personal statement in a one-on-one situation.

You should describe yourself honestly and completely. Programs and employers need and want people who have *particular traits* and *skills*. They can't conduct detailed interviews with all of their applicants. They rely on documents, like your personal statement, to see if you are the person they need. Giving them a laundry list of your accomplishments *does not* guarantee that they will recognize your strengths. You must organize and describe your attributes for them. The Personal Marketing Inventory will help you do this.

How to complete the Inventory

Depending on your goals and needs, you can complete the Personal Marketing Inventory in three ways, based on the amount of time and thought you want to invest.

- *Scan it.* Quickly read it, checking those areas that pertain directly to you. Then simply list the ones that you want to include in your personal statement.

- *Use specific topics.* Read through it and write down some ideas under the topics that are especially relevant to you. Use these in your personal statement.

- *Read it carefully.* Read the Inventory carefully and think about each topic. This method will be the most useful if you are struggling to write your personal statement or are relying heavily on your personal statement to secure the position you seek. The Inventory's questions present several different perspectives from which to view your experiences. This will increase your chances of remembering important events.

No matter which method you choose, use the examples to trigger your memory. Explain, in writing, your experiences under relevant categories and specify particular traits or skills that you developed as a result of these experiences. Be honest, and don't be shy.

Do you have trouble remembering what you did three years ago? Most of us do. Therefore, review the materials listed below *before* you complete the Personal Marketing Inventory.

- Your résumé (Chapter 4).

- Sample résumés (Chapter 5).

- Prior personal statements you have written, if any.

- Sample personal statements (Chapter 10).

Important points about the Inventory

Before beginning to work on your Personal Marketing Inventory, you need to understand some important points associated with its use.

- *Use the Personal Marketing Inventory.* While the Personal Marketing Inventory looks long, it should take you less than 45 minutes to complete. It appears long because it contains numerous examples to stimulate your memory and to illustrate how other individuals described their marketable attributes. You need similar descriptions in your personal statement.

- *Go through the Personal Marketing Inventory at least twice.* People often forget what they did during their first years of undergraduate and professional schools, or in their training programs. I find that going through the Personal Marketing Inventory at least twice, and sometimes a third or fourth time, often helps people remember additional experiences.

- *Some of the Inventory's items are repeated.* The Personal Marketing Inventory intentionally asks similar questions from slightly different perspectives. Thus, some of the items appear redundant. They are designed that way. Shifts in perspective can help jog your memory so that you don't forget important personal strengths. List both good and bad events. Coping with the challenges presented by unpleasant experiences must have taught you something useful.

- *Few people have responses for every item.* The items focus on specific academic, work-related, extracurricular, and personal issues that pertain to a broad range of people. Your background and experiences will determine those items that pertain to you. Ted, for example, had never traveled abroad, so that category was not relevant to him. However, he had extensive experience caring for animals. Specifically, he noted that he had cared for sick and injured pets that could not discuss their needs, and he had dealt with concerned pet owners. He referred to this background when he applied to pediatric residency programs. In short, he focused on what he had done rather than what he had not done. Like Ted, *focus on what you have done.*

- *List everything you can think of.* Don't limit yourself to the space given in this book. I expect that you will need lots of paper to list the myriad of events in your background. Buy a notebook and allocate several pages to each category. Remember, you will probably apply for many jobs during your career, and, as Chapter 12 points out, if you want to advance in your chosen profession, you must continue to develop new skills. A notebook you can keep adding things to will make it easy to update your résumé and personal statement.

- *You don't have to use all the things on your list.* Remember, however, that just because you list something on your Personal Marketing Inventory, doesn't mean you should include it in your personal statement or other application materials. Do not include a skill on your personal statement which you possess but do not wish to use. If it is mentioned, your employer will expect you to use that skill if asked. For example,

Jill listed Japanese among her language skills on both her résumé and personal statement. But she hated to translate Japanese for other people because it was extremely difficult. Soon after she was hired her new employer asked her to translate for a Japanese patient during a consultation. Jill refused, and her employer was extremely upset.

- *Skills and traits are different.* Traits are usually associated with behavior patterns. Being punctual or responsible, and always finishing what you begin are examples of traits. Skills refer to hands-on or procedural knowledge. Fluency in a language, mechanical ability, and operating x-ray equipment are all skills. You can have strengths in both areas, most people do. Employers, for example, like punctual workers (as do patients) and might be thrilled that you know how to fix intricate lab equipment.

Now complete your own Personal Marketing Inventory.

YOUR PERSONAL MARKETING INVENTORY

School-Based Experiences

List and describe any school-based experiences that shaped your life. Examples are *courses* and *extracurricular activities* that developed knowledge or abilities, such as discipline, leadership, problem-solving, or interpersonal skills.

- *Before and during high school.* While taking a required biology course, Scott became fascinated with genetics and read everything he could find on the field. He later completed advanced biology, received honors for a genetics science project, and decided to pursue a career in basic genetic research. Now, list your experiences.

_____

_____

_____

_____

_____

_____

_____

- *Undergraduate years.* Joycelyn was vice-president of her college's volunteer service club. She scheduled speakers for monthly meetings and coordinated volunteer activities for members, including a very successful student-run book exchange program. Describe experiences from your undergraduate years.

_____

_____

_____

_____

_____

_____

_____

- *Graduate school.* Andrea worked as a research assistant in her advisor's laboratory during graduate school. She learned valuable problem-solving, time management, and administrative skills. Andrea also learned to write research grants and articles for professional journals. Describe your experiences.

_____

_____

_____

_____

_____

_____

_____

_____

_____

_____

- *Health Professions school.* Faced with a heavier and more difficult work load than he had ever faced, Victor developed excellent study and work habits that he then taught to struggling classmates. Describe your experiences.

_____

_____

_____

_____

_____

_____

_____

_____

_____

_____

- *Residency/Fellowship training.* Darren and his advisor decided to prepare a case report of a rare disease. Darren was listed as an author on the published case and he presented it at a national meeting. He learned a great deal about the disease, the process of writing a case report, and how to speak before large audiences. Discuss your experiences.

_____

_____

_____

_____

_____

_____

_____

_____

Personal Experiences

List and describe any personal experiences that influenced your life in each category. These may have been pleasant (e.g., marriage or having a child) or challenging (e.g., illnesses or deaths of family members, divorce, or financial crisis). Describe how each event developed traits (e.g., persistence, discipline, or empathy) and improved your skills (e.g., leadership, communication, or money management). An example is provided under each category.

- *Through high school.* Walter volunteered in a pharmacy during his last two years in high school. He became friends with one pharmacist who was an outstanding role model. This man helped him learn some of the business and clinical aspects of pharmacy practice. Now, discuss your experiences.

_____

_____

_____

_____

_____

_____

_____

- *Undergraduate school.* Jay worked part-time as the fund-raising coordinator for a local charity. He polished his administrative and marketing skills while coordinating several major fund-raising events. Describe your experiences.

_____

_____

_____

_____

_____

_____

_____

_____

_____

_____

- *Graduate school.* Kathy tutored community college students in anatomy and physiology while completing her Ph.D. She said tutoring helped her realize how much she enjoyed teaching, and helped hone her teaching skills.

_____

_____

_____

_____

_____

_____

_____

_____

_____

- *Health Professions school.* Suzanne became friends with some elderly neighbors during her second year of school. When her neighbors' daughter died after a long battle with breast cancer, Suzanne supported them emotionally. Through this experience she learned of the needs close family members have when confronted with the loss of loved ones. She also became more comfortable with the subjects of death and dying.

_____

_____

_____

_____

_____

_____

_____

_____

_____

- *Residency/Fellowship training.* Cynthia became interested in computers during her last year of internal medicine residency. She polished her word processing skills, learned how to use a spreadsheet program, and prepared her own 35-mm slide shows using a presentation program. Describe your experiences.

_____

_____

_____

_____

_____

_____

_____

_____

_____

_____

_____

- *Other experiences.* Richard represented his county on the state's Emergency Medical Services advisory group while he was an assistant professor. He learned valuable negotiating and financial management skills during the budget discussions. He also gained insight into the political processes of the state and local governments. Discuss your experiences.

_____

_____

_____

_____

_____

_____

_____

_____

Professional/Clinical Interests

You probably have *professional* or *clinical* interests about which you enjoy reading or talking, or in which you have special expertise. As with Personal Interests, reviewers may share some of these with you.

Janice volunteered on a heart transplant team while in nursing school. In one case she flew to another city to obtain a harvested organ and she later observed the actual heart transplant operation. Her interest in surgery and transplantation grew throughout nursing school. When she applied for her first job, this interest was noted by several interviewers who shared similar experiences or interests.

- List any of your professional or clinical interests below.

_____

_____

_____

_____

_____

_____

_____

Work Experiences

Work experiences can significantly influence an individual. For example, Phyllis completed training as a Medical Technologist. She acquired significant experience while on the job. She said:

> I wasn't very sure of myself when I started my first job as a medical technologist. I gradually learned I could do the job, so my confidence increased. Over several years, the pathologist in charge of the lab gave me more responsibility and encouraged me to acquire extra skills. I learned how to better deal with patients, physicians, and administrators. I helped to develop new procedures and evaluate new tests. He suggested I think about getting a graduate degree. I started taking prerequisite courses, and I just took the GMAT. I'm going to get my Masters in Health Care Administration.

- List work experiences that significantly influenced you and describe the skills or traits they developed.

_____

_____

_____

_____

_____

_____

_____

_____

_____

_____

_____

_____

_____

_____

_____

_____

Volunteer Experiences

Volunteer experiences can also develop key abilities.

> Peter volunteered in a Miami, Florida emergency department. He quickly learned to assist the staff whenever he was needed, and he recognized how skillfully the physicians handled the worst trauma cases. He saw how different professionals contributed to patient care and realized that he wanted to become a physician. His experiences and new clinical skills helped him acquire a paid position in the hospital during his undergraduate years, and the physicians wrote letters of recommendation for him when he applied to medical school.

- Specify volunteer experiences you have had and describe the traits or skills they developed in you.

_____

_____

_____

_____

_____

_____

_____

_____

_____

_____

_____

_____

_____

Travel

Travel, in addition to being enjoyable, can also help you acquire or polish language skills, and develop a better understanding of health issues in other cultures. It also provides you with the opportunity to meet interesting people. You may have traveled because you like it, or you may have traveled out of necessity (e.g., family or religious obligations). "Travel" includes visits to other regions of the United States as well as to other countries. Sometimes the trials and tribulations accompanying travel can themselves be learning experiences.

Grace, now a family medicine resident, took a year off from medical school to travel to India to see how physicians there cared for their patients. Unfortunately, she was bitten by a stray dog on her second day in the country. She remarked that she will always remember her anxiety and the pain of that bite, as well as the quality of care and the compassion she received from the physician who treated her bite and gave her anti-rabies injections.

School-based travel opportunities can provide many meaningful experiences. For example, the International Health elective available at the University of Arizona College of Medicine exposes students from many schools to a wide range of health and cultural issues as they complete required projects.

Rosa took this elective and completed a research project that determined how people in a Mexican border town stored drinking water. Rosa became more fluent in Spanish, increased her understanding of the culture, and honed her research skills while she completed her elective. She subsequently presented her research findings at local and national conferences. These experiences, in turn, helped her to develop her public speaking skills.

- List the places to which you have traveled. For each place, describe any unique experiences that occurred, how they influenced you, and the skills you developed during the experience.

_____

_____

_____

_____

_____

_____

_____

_____

_____

_____

_____

_____

_____

Inter-Cultural Experiences

Have you experienced different cultures, either by traveling to a different country or by interacting at home with people from other cultures? For example, health professions students can meet Hispanics and native Americans, among others, in the southwestern United States. Many students have experienced personal and professional growth and gained valuable insights when their world view expanded.

> Bradley, now a dental student, worked assisting a nurse practitioner in an Indian Health Service hospital in northern Arizona. In addition to learning about and experiencing the native American culture, Bradley found that the rich, ancient Hopi culture offered new insights to him on life, death, and the individual's place in his society and the world.

- Identify any experiences with people from other cultures that have significantly influenced you.

_____

_____

_____

_____

_____

_____

_____

_____

_____

_____

_____

_____

_____

Languages

The ability to speak a language in addition to English has become increasingly important in the medical environment. A physician in a large California hospital public health clinic recently told me of the wide variety of languages spoken by her patients. Being able to communicate with these patients and their family members (she speaks three languages plus English) has been a real asset in her practice. You can use your language ability as a major strength in your marketing plan.

Some people hesitate to claim facility in another language unless they can speak and write it fluently. Frankly, this is a judgment call. I don't believe that you need to speak a language fluently in order to record it as a second language. You should, however, know it well enough to communicate basic information relevant to the position for which you are applying. For example, physicians, dentists and nurses should have specific experience taking medical histories and giving physical examinations using that language.

People reading your personal statement want to know: Do you speak a language, in addition to English, well enough to carry on a basic conversation? If so, what is the language? How well do you speak or write it? Can you take a history and perform a physical exam in that language? Is that language frequently spoken in the area where you live now or wish to practice in the future?

Speaking English. One important caveat. English remains the common medical language in the United States. Applicants whose first language is not English, *must* speak English well enough to be understood by patients and colleagues. They must also be able to understand others speaking colloquial English. (Sometimes even people from Britain, Australia, and New Zealand have difficulties with American English.) Reviewers consider this of paramount importance. If you can tell them that you have excellent facility with English, you stand a better chance of getting your foot in the door.

- List your language skills. An example is given.

Language	Ability to Use	Use in Health Fields
Chinese	Fluent in Cantonese	Often took histories and performed physicals in Cantonese during school.

Teaching Experiences

Many positions may require that you serve as an instructor for students, residents, new people on the job, or the public. Even students may need to instruct some groups, including more junior students. Teachers, through necessity, learn tolerance, patience, and the ability to explain difficult concepts clearly.

> Stephanie taught sex education and AIDS awareness to junior high-age inner-city youth while she was in college. She received a service award for this activity saying how well she related to the children.

Not all teaching experiences result from formal programs.

> Greg did particularly well in his chemistry classes. Many of his dorm-mates didn't do so well and relied on Greg to informally tutor them. He became so well-known for doing this that he was offered a formal tutoring job, which he declined.

- Describe your own teaching experiences and explain how each helped you develop specific skills or traits.

_____

_____

_____

_____

_____

_____

_____

_____

_____

_____

_____

_____

_____

_____

Research Experiences

Research experiences can be valuable marketing points, especially if the requirements of the position for which you are applying either include or suggest prior completion of research projects. If you have participated in a research study, you probably learned that research has its ups and downs. You may have learned a great deal about problem-solving, time management, and budgeting. In addition, you probably experienced frustrations with delays, unexpected results, botched experiments, and financial constraints.

> Alan, a dental student, carefully planned his research elective. Yet he quickly became frustrated after learning that he needed additional funds to use a sophisticated centrifuge. Unfortunately, he didn't have time to write a grant to acquire the funds. He finally considered his options and realized that he had to abandon his project temporarily. He chose instead to participate in a faculty member's project that had already been funded. Alan enjoyed the project and learned, among other things, that research is hard work, has unexpected roadblocks, and doesn't always result in startling discoveries.

Remember that *even if* no publications or presentations result from the research, you have most likely acquired skills and traits from the experience. You may cite research experiences (but *not* publications or presentations) on your résumé or personal statement even if your name did not appear among the authors or presenters.

> Nancy worked in her undergraduate advisor's laboratory during her sophomore year. She learned to conduct literature searches, evaluate articles, and follow her advisor's instructions. Although her name never appeared among the authors' names on the publications that resulted from the experiments, she did acquire valuable experiences that she can translate into marketable skills.

- Have you ever conducted or participated in a research study? What attributes (i.e., time management, problem-solving, or computer skills) did the experience help you develop? List these.

_____

_____

_____

_____

_____

_____

_____

_____

Academic /Job-Related Accomplishments

You may have excelled academically in classroom-based courses or in clinical rotations. You may also have excelled on the job and received glowing performance evaluations. These are extremely important because they suggest future performance at the same level. Point these out to selection committees.

> Juanita entered dental school after working as a dental hygienist. She received "excellent" performance ratings on the job. Her academic performance in her basic science courses was acceptable, but not stellar, largely because she worked extensively as a hygienist during those years. She subsequently quit her outside job, blossomed in her clinical courses, and earned "honors" in each one–a rare accomplishment. Initially, Juanita was reluctant to view her academic accomplishments as marketable attributes. Eventually though, she decided to mention her accomplishments, while giving credit to the faculty, on her personal statement. She also mentioned her job performance ratings.

- Describe situations in which you have excelled academically in the classroom, in clinical rotations, or in job ratings. For each instance, describe *how* you achieved this accomplishment.

_____

_____

_____

_____

_____

_____

_____

_____

_____

_____

_____

_____

_____

_____

_____

Hobbies

You may have a hobby, such as woodworking, painting, stamp collecting, acting, or repairing VCRs that has helped you polish existing skills or develop new abilities. You may have been naturally inclined toward your hobby and may even still be involved in it. It is highly possible that people on selection committees have similar hobbies to yours. Shared hobbies are like magnets–they can increase your attraction to these people.

John, now applying for a bioengineering position, from an early age liked to disassemble alarm clocks (sometimes he could even reassemble them) and build model cars and planes. He still builds and flies radio-controlled planes as a hobby. As a result, he has highly developed his hand-eye coordination. He hopes to use this skill in developing automated laboratory equipment.

Charles' father always had encouraged him to help with his woodworking projects. Charles became increasingly skilled at building ornate furniture. While interviewing for a residency in orthopedic surgery, he found that several people who interviewed him also had woodworking as their hobbies. They discussed this mutual interest during the interviews.

Maria Lopez, a vivacious and outgoing medical student, was active in the theater while in undergraduate school. Maria recognized that although her outgoing personality had initially facilitated her participation in productions, she had also developed numerous other skills such as writing and directing. Her unique personal statement (see Chapter 10, statement #16), a script of an interview between a program director and herself, expertly displayed these talents.

- If you have a hobby, list it and describe particular skills or abilities it has helped you polish or develop.

_____

_____

_____

_____

_____

_____

_____

_____

_____

Sports-Related Interests

You may enjoy, or be especially gifted in, one or more sports like softball, snow skiing, ice-skating, running, hiking, or swimming. You may have even been recognized by others for these abilities. Sports can help develop leadership, communication skills, and discipline–all highly desirable and marketable qualities.

> Darlene and her spouse were avid spelunkers (cavers). She described how the sport had taught her mind and body control, the need for careful planning, and how to both rely on team members and be responsible for others' safety. These experiences contributed to her being a much sought-after applicant.

- Think of your sports interests. Write them down and describe the traits/abilities each developed in you.

_____

_____

_____

_____

_____

_____

_____

_____

_____

_____

_____

Personal Interests

You probably have interests and activities outside the health sciences that you enjoy. Others may share those interests with you, and shared interests are great ice-breakers!

> Annette, a department chairman, recently told me about someone who interviewed for a faculty position in her department. Bill used part of his personal statement to describe his interest in sailing. Annette said that she immediately felt a connection with him because of this shared interest. She and Bill discussed the topic during his interview. This made the interview easier for both Annette and Bill.

> Jeff, a paramedic, volunteered with a local wilderness search and rescue team. He participated in many wilderness rescues involving

technical climbing and rescue techniques. He performed medical procedures in the field which were seldom used by his peers in urban settings. One reviewer was a rock climber himself, and called Jeff for an interview. He was looking for paramedics with wilderness medical experience, and was delighted to gain a potential climbing partner as well.

- What interests do you enjoy reading or talking about? List them below.

_____

_____

_____

_____

_____

_____

_____

_____

_____

_____

Other Significant Experiences

You may have been motivated or stimulated by some other significant experience which hasn't been covered so far. Although an experience may seem trivial to you, others who have had similar experiences will easily relate to its potential influence on you. Including these experiences may create common bonds between you and reviewers. Besides, the memory of these experiences might also remind you why you chose to pursue a health professions career.

Experiences may be *positive* or *negative*. You may have had a positive experience by observing a role model whom you want to emulate.

Tim's uncle practiced dentistry in a small town. Tim saw how others respected him and how thoughtfully his uncle cared for his patients. During high school and college Tim watched his uncle treat patients, gradually realizing that dentistry was the ultimate calling for him. His uncle encouraged Tim to become a dentist.

You may also have been influenced by a negative experience.

Julie, as a law enforcement officer, watched helplessly as one of her fellow officers lay bleeding after he was shot. She traveled with him to a hospital's Emergency Department where she was especially impressed by the demeanor and skill of the attending surgeon. After that experience, Julie evaluated her career plans and returned to school to become a surgeon. Today Julie is a surgery resident. (See Chapter 10, statement # 24.)

Experiences may consist of a *critical incident* or a *series of events* that influenced you. Julie's experience of helplessly watching her wounded colleague was a critical incident in her life.

The influence of a series of events is illustrated by Faye, who volunteered in a student-run refugee clinic during nursing school. She became especially interested in the violence these refugees had endured in their home countries. Faye realized that although she could help them individually with many of their medical needs, they still had group needs that she was unable to address. She decided that she needed to enhance her public health background by completing a Master of Public Health program after nursing school.

Assess any positive or negative experiences that have shaped your life. Think about "critical incidents" as well as a long-term series of events that motivated you to attend a health professions school or to follow the specific career path you have chosen. List these events and describe how they affected you and your decision to pursue a health professions career.

_____

_____

_____

_____

_____

_____

_____

_____

_____

_____

Refer to the material you just finished. You can see how you have developed as a person and as a health-care provider. You only need to express this growth in your personal statement so that others can understand and relate to you as a unique individual who can contribute to their program or institution. Chapter 8 will help you do this. Turn to it now. The hard part is behind you. Go on! You are doing just fine.

8: Developing Your Marketing Strategy

Construct a personal statement that displays your talents.

Express your attributes in concrete terms

The Personal Marketing Inventory in Chapter 7 helped you assess your experiences. Now state your marketable attributes *in concrete terms*. Focus on skills and traits reviewers seek, so that you can use specific examples in your personal statement. You will match your strengths with the reviewers list from Chapter 6 to develop your marketing strategy. Then you will write your personal statement to show them that *you* match their criteria by clearly specifying your traits, values, skills, and experiences.

You have many worthwhile attributes that programs are seeking in their applicants. From all of your attributes, zero-in on those you want to list and describe in your personal statement. It is difficult to specify how many attributes you should discuss, but any more than ten may seem more like a laundry list of accomplishments than a personal statement.

Here are examples of some marketable attributes and ways you may have acquired or polished them:

- *Leadership skills.* Did you develop leadership skills as a class or organization officer, or as supervisor of the X-ray lab?

- *Possible future practice location.* Did you grow up in a rural or urban environment to which you want to return?

- *Hands-on skills.* Did you disassemble clocks or build things as a child? Do you have a hobby that requires you to perform fine-motor movements?

- *Team-building skills.* Did you play team sports or participate in club activities? Were you the chair of a committee?

- *Language skills.* Did speaking Russian fluently help you with patients while you worked as a respiratory therapist?

- *Empathy.* Do you better understand a patient or family member's perspective because of a personal experience with trauma or chronic illness?

- *Organizational skills.* Did serving in the military or as a class or club officer help develop your organizational skills?

- *Exposure to future demands.* Did you scrub-in on weekend surgeries during your first and second years in medical school to learn what surgeons really do? Did you spend time on administrative duties during residency training?

- *Teaching Skills.* Did you learn to run projectors or audiovisual equipment? Can you explain difficult concepts so that others can easily understand them? Did you tutor friends in school?

- *Demonstrating a long-term interest in a career.* Did you work in a local pharmacy as a pharmacy technician or in a hospital as a nurse's aide?

- *Building a knowledge base over time.* Did you attend ENT conferences throughout medical school to learn more about this specialty?

- *Ability to work under stress.* Did working as an emergency medical technician teach you to think quickly and perform under pressure?

Scan your completed Personal Marketing Inventory (Chapter 7). Identify the qualifications (strengths) you possess to include in your personal statement. Specify below the major points (e.g., marketable skills, traits, experiences) that you want reviewers to know about *you*. Be specific, giving an example for each strength. Programs and employers want traits like discipline and honesty, as well as administrative, research, leadership, and communication skills.

Remember that you may need one list for each job or program. If you need help, talk to your mentor/advisor. An example is given below.

Applicant: "Volunteering in a refugee clinic improved my Spanish."

Point 1: _____

Point 2: _____

Point 3: _____

Point 4: _____

Point 5: _____

Point 6: _____

Point 7: _____

Point 8: _____

Point 9: _____

You should now have a list of all of your marketable skills and traits. You need to focus only on the most valuable of these in your personal statement. But how do you choose those? It's easy. You just match your skills with those reviewers seek. Once you do that you will know your marketing strategy.

1. Using the list from Chapter 6, list three factors that people reviewing applications seek in applicants. Do this for each position you desire, as well as for each program or institution.

    1. _____

    2. _____

    3. _____

2. List the three most important qualities you want to emphasize in your personal statement so the selection committee can get to know *you*, the applicant.

    1. _____

    2. _____

    3. _____

Compare the lists

The lists you just made should share some common points. These commonalties are the "match" between you and the position. Don't misinterpret my goal. I am *not* advocating trying to play mind games with reviewers. Instead, I want to ensure that there is a good match between what they want in a candidate and what you, the candidate, have to offer. After you find each match, you must emphasize it in your personal statement written for that position. Matches like the ones below are great!

Readers:	We want physical therapists who can speak/learn Spanish.
Writer:	Volunteering in a clinic helped me become fluent in Spanish.
Readers:	We want department heads who can solve problems.
Writer:	My work on research projects developed my problem-solving skills.
Readers:	We want medical students who will practice in underserved areas.
Writer:	I grew up on a ranch in Montana. I experienced first-hand the health care needs of rural life. I want to practice medicine in a rural, medically underserved area.

List the matches (common areas) from the lists you just completed. You may need to do this for *each* position, program, or institution. You must realize that even if you are applying for a similar position at more than one institution (e.g., Medical Technologist in a Hematology lab), each institution may value different abilities. This will be due to their size, location, the patient population, range of diseases seen, and other factors.

Readers: _____

_____

You: _____

_____

Readers: _____

_____

You: _____

_____

Let's see how one applicant used this process.

Trevor, an applicant for a physician assistant program, had extensive clinical experience from his Navy medical training. He had not, however, excelled in some prerequisite coursework because he had had to work to pay for his son's unexpected medical expenses. Trevor decided that his marketable attributes were clinical experience and team-building skills. He talked to some program faculty and graduates, and learned that the admissions committee carefully screened applicants to ensure that they possessed the necessary background knowledge and skills. The committee also valued clinical experience highly. Trevor decided to explain in his personal statement how personal issues, now resolved, had adversely affected his academic work. In addition, he emphasized his clinical experience, a

"Must" for the program. Trevor also discussed his interpersonal skills—being able to get along with people from different cultures in trying circumstances—because this seemed to be a reasonable program "Want" for applicants.

Remember that matches are the Velcro strips that catch people and keep them in educational programs and career positions. The more matches between you and the program or institution to which you are applying, the greater the likelihood that they will select you. Better still, a high number of matches increases the likelihood that you will enjoy being there.

Dealing with mismatches

Sometimes mismatches may occur between the qualifications the selection committee wants in an applicant and what you, the applicant, have to offer. While qualifications seldom match in every specific area, certain types of mismatches can present real problems. Consider the example below.

Readers: We want physicians to conduct research and publish articles.
Writer: I'm a 'people' person. I want to treat patients, not conduct research.

Is this a mismatch? Yes it is. The readers' expectation and the applicant's desire with regard to research don't match.

Can mismatches present problems? Yes. If selected, the writer above may not be happy at that institution.

Mismatches can present short- or long-term problems.

> Matt, a person with a pre-med degree, applied for admission to a physical therapy program. The program's selection committee wanted students who would work in that field for some time. Matt's goal was to gain experience in the medical field before applying to medical school. He clearly stated that he had no desire to pursue a career in physical therapy. His fellow applicants had much less college experience, but all emphasized that they wanted careers in physical therapy. The committee noted the mismatch, but voted to enroll Matt. Shortly after classes began, conflicts occurred between Matt and his peers and the faculty. He eventually quit the program.

Significant mismatches merit attention. If there appears to be a mismatch between you and a position you are seeking, talk with your faculty or mentors. Sometimes mismatches can be resolved. For example, the "people person" who doesn't want to conduct research might thoroughly enjoy clinical research. Rosa (mentioned earlier), who is now a resident in Family Medicine, gained extensive clinical research experience by determining how people in one town in Mexico stored their drinking water. She found that water was stored in a variety of containers, some of which were old 55-gallon cans that had previously housed hazardous materials. She presented the results of this fascinating study at local and national conferences. Many other people have participated in interesting and productive studies that involve patients and their families. Consider these types of activities before you decide to avoid research just because you are a "people person."

Write the mismatches from the lists you just completed.

Readers: _____

_____

You: _____

_____

Readers: _____

_____

You: _____

_____

At this point you should have identified your marketable strengths that selection committees want in applicants. *You will use this list of marketable strengths in Chapter 9 as you write your personal statement.* You should also have identified any mismatches between your goals/strengths and a program's Musts/Wants. Evaluate these apparent mismatches and talk with a mentor to resolve them before you write your personal statement.

Addressing other issues

At times individuals are concerned about some aspect of their performance or behavior in the past that doesn't fit under a strength or a mismatch.

> David was a fourth-year student who performed well during his first year of osteopathic studies, but struggled academically during his second year because of his mother's terminal illness. He was concerned about explaining the drop in his grades. He asked, "Should I mention my low grades in my personal statement?"

You may have concerns about similar issues. Your personal statement is the only place (before an interview) that you have to explain them, and to describe how you responded to challenges. But to do that, you need to identify the pertinent issues and their related backgrounds. Then, you must view them from a different perspective. Examples of such issues include:

- Repeating a course or an entire year in school.

- Scoring low or failing a standardized test (e.g., MCAT, USMLE, NBEOPS).

- Poor evaluations in courses or clerkships.

- Chronic health problems.

Your concerns may be realistic or they may be blown out of proportion. Glaring discrepancies will stand out to reviewers. Mary Ann had to repeat each exam that she took during her third year of medical school, but she received glowing clinical evaluations. Her Dean's letter stated that she "did not test well." It is likely that a perceptive reviewer would notice this discrepancy–others might not, remembering only the low scores. If you suspect something like a low or failing score on the MCAT or a licensure exam could adversely affect you, discuss your concerns with an advisor or mentor. Avoid negative self-talk like, "I'll never get into medical school after getting a 'C' in Organic Chemistry." It won't help you deal with the issue. Instead, first determine to what extent a problem really exists. Then decide if it needs to be addressed and how to approach it in your personal statement (or during an interview if an interviewer introduces the topic).

1. *Assess your concerns.* Think about any problems. Discuss them with a mentor or advisor to better determine how they might affect your consideration by a prospective employer. You can acquire information about entrance requirements for programs from their admissions/selection personnel. If you are applying for medical school, for example, ask about the range of MCAT scores in their current class. If you are applying for a residency program, talk to faculty to learn about program selection criteria and get a realistic appraisal of your strengths from a mentor who knows you well. For jobs, find out what experience level they require.

2. *Decide which issues to address.* Some problems, like chronic health conditions or substance abuse, are very personal and should be addressed very diplomatically (if at all) with the guidance of a mentor or advisor. For example, Connie, a recovering alcoholic, was applying to a large hospital as an attending physician. She wanted to inform the administrator directly of her past history of substance abuse, but was concerned that such a disclosure would keep her from being hired. After talking with a mentor, Connie decided to address the issue as a chronic health problem.

   The point is that certain disclosures may, in fact, keep you from getting the position you desire. You should discuss your concerns with your advisor or mentor. If that person doesn't help, get a second opinion. Issues like a failed course or low "board" score can be understood, especially if you have a valid explanation of what happened and how you addressed the problem. Others, such as substance abuse, should be carefully evaluated to decide if and how to disclose and explain the problem. Be honest, but don't divulge highly personal and sensitive information without getting the advice of someone you trust.

3. *Address issues from a positive perspective.* After you identify the problem and assess its possible impact, try to think about it from a different perspective. This will help you when you address it in your personal statement or during an interview.

   Stan, now a family medicine resident, had to repeat the first two exams he took during his third year in medical school. After two re-takes, he changed his study habits and completed the remainder of his exams on the first attempt. Stan decided to address this issue indirectly on his personal statement. He emphasized *how* he had adapted his learning techniques to fit the fast-paced, clinical learning environment.

Emphasize what you learned from bad situations. Don't try to avoid responsibility for problems. Simply explain what happened, how you solved the problem, and what you learned from the experience. For example,

Instead of: My grades dropped during my senior year in college.

Say: Although distracted by my father's death during my senior year in college, I passed all my courses. That experience gave me insight into how a patient's illness and death may affect his spouse and children.

Now list any concerns you believe you must address in your personal statement:

_____

_____

_____

_____

Assess your strengths again

Now, review the points you initially wanted to emphasize in your personal statement. Do you still wish to emphasize the same points? Record any additions and deletions here. Briefly describe why you are making a change.

_____

_____

_____

Writing your personal statement

Congratulations! You have completed your Personal Marketing Inventory and developed your marketing strategy. You are ready to write your personal statement. You should have a pool of marketable traits that, like Velcro, will stick in the reviewers' minds after they read your personal statement. In addition, your ego should be bolstered somewhat now that you realize that you *do* possess skills and traits that programs and employers seek!

Chapter 9 provides a step-by-step writing plan. It shows you how to distill these marketable traits down to one polished page. Keep going, you're almost done!

9: Writing Your Personal Statement: A Step-by-Step Plan

Follow the plan–stay on the path–and you won't get lost.

Overview

This chapter will help you *write a personal statement that describes your marketable attributes and helps the reader know you as a person.* There is no "ideal" format for personal statements. Organize yours to fit your own style. Most people write narratives which emphasize their key attributes. Others use different approaches.

Maria Lopez, who majored in dramatic arts in undergraduate school, wrote a very different personal statement for her family medicine residency application (see Chapter 10, statement # 16). Her personal statement is a script depicting an interview between her and a residency director. This personal statement met the goal, as described above, because it portrayed her as she really was.

Most people need a strategy to write an effective personal statement. Otherwise, they get "bogged down" and frustrated. You used the Personal Marketing Inventory to identify your marketable attributes. Now, you must simply distill these attributes down to one well-written page. This chapter *will give you a writing strategy* to do this. An overview of that strategy, "The Forest," is presented first. Then, "The Trees" explains and illustrates each step of the strategy. As you write, refer to the examples of personal statements in Chapter 10.

Remember, as you read this chapter, your goal is to write a personal statement that depicts *you*. You can't go wrong with that!

The Forest: A step-by-step writing strategy

Writing a powerful personal statement takes time, thought, and several revisions. The steps below will help you organize your ideas and write a polished personal statement. Many of these steps mimic the strategies effective writers use to get their ideas into print. An overview of these steps (the "forest") is presented below.

1. Read the sample personal statements in Chapter 10.
2. Determine the traits and skills selection committees seek.
3. Identify your marketable attributes.
4. Compare the lists from 2 and 3 above for matches and discrepancies.
5. Identify attributes to emphasize in your personal statement.
6. Outline your personal statement paragraph by paragraph.
7. Write a topic sentence for each paragraph.
8. Write the first draft.

   Ensure that each sentence supports the topic (main idea) sentence.

   Write forceful, active, varied, and understandable sentences.
9. Get feedback.
10. Revise as needed.
11. Check the final copy for grammatical and spelling errors.
12. Print and *send* it. At some point you have to stop revising. It will never be perfect, but it must be received by the reviewers to do its job for you.
13. If you are applying for more than one type of program or position, repeat the process for each one. I cannot recommend using a generic personal statement in this situation.

THE TREES: STEPS FOR WRITING A PERSONAL STATEMENT

The rest of this chapter explains and illustrates how to use each step (the "trees"). Check-off each step ☑ as you proceed through the list.

❏ 1. *Read sample personal statements.* Reading examples is an excellent way to start the writing process. They illustrate how other writers have provided readers with a picture of themselves as individuals. After reading the examples in Chapter 10 or those of friends and associates, answer these questions.

- *What impresses you about each personal statement?* A well-written personal statement leaves readers with a favorable impression. It gives them a "window" into the writer's mind. This window lets them "meet" the authors by reading about their personal lives–their attributes, goals, and the experiences that shaped them. In other words, they learn about the authors as people– something they can't get from transcripts. Read several personal statements and list what made each stand out for you. Notice how you were attracted to some writers. What attracted you? What key points do you remember about each statement? What would you talk about if you were to interview a particular writer?

- *How are the statements unique and different?* Well-written personal statements are unique, because no two people have the same experiences, attributes, and goals. Since there is no "ideal" personal statement format, use one that will best reflect your marketable attributes, goals, and personal style. Read and synthesize ideas from other personal statements, but never try to duplicate another person's personal statement–this will sound phony. Read some personal statements and think about what made each one unique.

- *How do writers directly and indirectly emphasize their marketable attributes?* Some writers directly state an attribute, such as:

  "The research experience developed my problem-solving skills."

  Others indirectly state their strengths. What *five* attributes did the writer below indirectly describe in this one sentence?

  "I enjoyed volunteering in our medical students' Refugee Clinic because I enjoy meeting patients from other cultures, working with my classmates, and speaking Spanish."

Follow this rule: Directly state something if you really want to emphasize your point! Indirectly state it if the direct account sounds too pompous.

- *What attracted you to some personal statements?* Many people in specialized areas (e.g., pediatrics) share common interests and personality traits. Attract readers to yourself by describing the personal attributes that you probably share with them. Common interests are "ice-breakers" that personalize you and make you seem like a friend rather than a total stranger.

131

- *Let your personal statement do its job.* Did you notice that some personal statements appealed to you more than others? Some may not have appealed to you at all. That's normal. In fact, that's desirable. You want to honestly describe the *real* you. It's a "win-win" situation when your experiences, attributes, and goals match those desired by a program or employer. However, it is also a "win-win" situation if the reviewer sees the mismatch between you and the position. Both you and the institution win because the institution saves an interview slot and you save money, time, and the possible misfortune of getting a position that you will not like.

☐ 2. *Determine which skills or traits you possess that selection committees are seeking.* In Chapter 6 you identified what reviewers are looking for in applicants. Some attributes they seek are "Musts," while others are "Wants." Be sure you have developed your own lists of the skills and traits reviewers who will read your application materials are seeking before preceding.

☐ 3. *Identify your marketable attributes.* In Chapter 7 you identified and listed the specific attributes (e.g., leadership skills, goals) that you possess. Then, in Chapter 8 you listed qualities you want reviewers to know about you. Your goal now is to describe yourself honestly and accurately. Look over the lists you made and fine-tune them. If you have a question about an attribute you think you possess, talk about it with your mentor or advisor. Think about what makes *you unique.* Be specific.

> Initially, Andy described himself as "bright, hard-working, and a nice person." All of that was true, but it also described almost every other applicant. I encouraged Andy to focus on his unique attributes, like his long-term interest in research illustrated by his completing a research project following his first year in medical school.

☐ 4. *Develop your marketing strategy.* As you did in Chapter 8, compare the lists from 2 and 3 above for matches and discrepancies. Hopefully, the lists will have many common points. Emphasize those in your personal statement. Note any discrepancies or "mismatches" and discuss them with your mentor or advisor. If there is a "mismatch" in either yours or a potential employer's "Must" area, definitely resolve it *before* writing your personal statement.

☐ 5. *Identify attributes to emphasize in your personal statement.* Your personal statement, in addition to containing your attributes, should help the reader understand how you developed them. Go for a manageable number of attributes and experiences so they will "stick like Velcro" to the readers' minds as they screen, interview, and select applicants. (The attributes Andy decided to emphasize are underlined in the outline in the next section.)

This step concludes the preliminary work. You should have identified your strengths–the ones reviewers want–already, and decided upon a marketing strategy. Now, let's get them on paper!

☐ 6. *Outline your personal statement paragraph by paragraph.* Most people have trouble organizing their personal statements. You need a framework to organize and present your attributes. One way to build a framework is to divide your personal statement into five or six paragraphs. Then, decide what you want to emphasize in each paragraph. For example, read the outline of Andy's personal statement below. Notice how Andy underlined the attributes he wanted to emphasize.

> *Paragraph 1*: Catch the reader's attention and emphasize my <u>long-term interest in medicine and orthopedic surgery</u> by describing volunteer/work experiences.

> *Paragraph 2*: Describe <u>leadership</u> and <u>organizational skills</u> and <u>science background</u> I gained through specific undergraduate academic and extracurricular experiences.

> *Paragraph 3*: Describe my <u>knowledge base</u> developed through basic science courses and clinical clerkships, and my <u>problem-solving</u> and <u>computer skills</u> acquired through the Medical Student Research Program.

> *Paragraph 4*: Describe why I want to be an orthopedic surgeon and relate this goal to my <u>physical abilities</u>.

> *Paragraph 5*: Describe my <u>sports interests</u> and <u>hobbies</u> (woodworking and playing the guitar). Note how my <u>spouse</u> provided emotional support throughout medical school.

> *Paragraph 6*: Maintain the readers' attention by stating my <u>goals</u> and describing what I'm seeking in a program–like a <u>diverse patient population</u>, <u>teaching and research opportunities</u>, and a <u>team atmosphere</u>.

Two things are important about your outline. First, *catch the reader's attention in Paragraph 1*. Attention-catching techniques include describing an exciting incident, relating a personal story, or discussing how you became interested in your career field. Sure, they might sound mundane to you, but use one of these or a similar approach to grab the reader's attention.

Second, *emphasize the attributes you seek* in a program or position. Diverse patient populations, varied cases, on-line faculty teaching, urban or rural settings, opportunities to conduct research, teach, or use a specific language are some points you can specify. Help the reviewers evaluate the "position-to-applicant" match. *Don't* tailor this paragraph to each program or try to "play up to" readers. For example, one student's personal statement contained the sentence below in the final paragraph.

"I really like your program at Mission Valley Medical Center. Of all the programs I have read about, it is the best."

This sentence illustrates at least two problems. First, most application reviewers know how easy it is to change a few words with a word processor. They will assume that you changed the sentence for every institution to which you applied. That makes you look like insincere (which you undoubtedly are not). The second problem is that occasionally applicants put personal statements in with the wrong applications during the often-frantic mailing process. This happens more often than you might think. If it happens to a personal statement containing a sentence like Andy's above, the applicant would most likely be eliminated from consideration at *both* programs. Personalize your statement by writing about yourself, not by mentioning the program.

Now, outline your personal statement below. Underline the personal attributes and experiences you want to discuss to insure you include them all.

PARAGRAPH	Attributes and experiences to emphasize
1.	_____
	_____
	_____
2.	_____
	_____
	_____
3.	_____
	_____
	_____
4.	_____
	_____
	_____
5.	_____
	_____
	_____
6.	_____
	_____
	_____

❐ 7. *Write a topic sentence for each paragraph.* A topic sentence contains the paragraph's main idea. It tells readers what the paragraph is about. You may recall that a topic sentence can appear at the beginning, middle, or end of a paragraph. The other sentences in a paragraph support the topic sentence. Don't take chances: *Place the topic sentence at the beginning of each paragraph* to ensure that the reader knows the main idea of each paragraph. Read the following paragraph from a personal statement. The topic sentence is underlined.

> <u>Fully using my talents and abilities to benefit others is an integral part of the ideals my family instilled in me.</u> I was reared in a close-knit extended family that always supported and nurtured me and used the achievements of one member to inspire a celebration for all. My parents have always been active in various community organizations and have encouraged me to do the same. While in high school I shadowed physicians who volunteered their time at the St. Vincent de Paul Clinic, a facility that serves the indigent population of Cincinnati. At the Ohio Upward Foundation I worked with mentally challenged children. Since all of my grandparents are still alive and quite active, I have always enjoyed spending time with older people. This led me to volunteer at a residential community for the elderly.

Read the two paragraphs below and notice the difference between them. Paragraph A's topic sentence (underlined) is in the last part of the paragraph. Paragraph B's is the first sentence. Which paragraph is easier to understand?

Paragraph A

The physical and emotional strain of a difficult pregnancy and family illness tested my learning and coping skills. Less than three weeks after the birth of my son, I completed the fall semester of my second year. I learned first-hand that juggling the rigors of school and parenthood required organization and flexibility. Supporting my mother-in-law through her progressing dementia has made Alzheimer's emotional toll on a patient's loved ones very real to me. A close-knit family and stable home life have allowed me to complete medical school with my original classmates. <u>Thus, medical school has been a time of profound intellectual and personal growth.</u>

Paragraph B

<u>Medical school has been a time of profound intellectual and personal growth.</u> The physical and emotional strain of a difficult pregnancy and family illness tested my learning and coping skills. Less than three weeks after the birth of my son, I completed the fall semester of my second year. I learned first-hand that juggling the rigors of school and parenthood required organization and flexibility. Supporting my mother-in-law through her progressing dementia has made Alzheimer's emotional toll on a patient's loved ones very real to me. A

close-knit family and stable home life have allowed me to complete medical school with my original classmates.

Was the location of the topic sentence important? In general, putting the topic sentence last (for variety) is best used in fiction and long non-fiction pieces. Strive to make your personal statement understandable and easy to read.

Now, write a topic sentence for each of your paragraphs.

1. _____
   _____

2. _____
   _____

3. _____
   _____

4. _____
   _____

5. _____
   _____

6. _____
   _____

☐ 8. *Write the first draft.* This is the hard part. Sit down and begin writing. It's important that you get your ideas on paper. Don't worry about how much you write. Remember, this is only a draft. Make sure you write and revise your personal statement using a word processing program. Typing or writing in long-hand is not the best way to use your time and will dissuade you from doing the necessary revisions. If necessary, get a friend or professional typing service to enter your draft into the computer, then edit. The following hints will make writing a bit easier. See Figure 9.1 for a first draft with comments.

Ensure that other sentences in a paragraph support the topic (main idea) sentence. Each paragraph should contain *one* topic sentence and *one or more* supporting sentences. Make sure each supporting sentence is related to the idea stressed in your topic sentence. For example, in Paragraph B, above, notice how the other sentences support the topic sentence.

Write *forceful*, *active*, *varied*, and *understandable* sentences. Clear, declarative sentences can be read quickly and easily, and they are less open to individual interpretation. The example sentences below illustrate first drafts (poor use) and final versions (good use) of each principle.

- *Forceful* sentences demonstrate confidence. They let the reader know you are ready for action. They are direct and definite about your ability to do something.

  Draft: I think I possess qualities needed to become a surgeon.

  Final: I possess the skills and knowledge to become an excellent surgeon.

- *Active* sentences use action verbs. Avoid passive verbs. Words like 'be', 'is', 'are', 'am', and 'to' often indicate a passive sentence. Look at the examples below, check your sentences, and revise as needed.

  Draft: A residency program that will provide a broad-based clinical experience with a diverse patient population is desired by me.

  Final: I seek a residency program that provides a broad-based clinical experience with a diverse patient population.

- *Varied* sentences keep the reader's attention. Use different sentence lengths and styles, as well as different words. Avoid over-using words, abbreviations, or pronouns (I, me, etc.).

  Draft: My parents emigrated from Spain. They always encouraged me to experience other cultures. I spent the summer of 1989 in Spain. I polished my Spanish and met many new friends. I also traveled through France and learned French. I still enjoy hiking and traveling to new places.

  Final: My parents, immigrants from Spain, always encouraged me to experience other cultures. I spent the summer of 1989 in Spain, where I polished my Spanish and met many new friends. Later, I traveled through France and learned French. I still enjoy hiking and traveling to new places.

- *Understandable* sentences are easy to read and comprehend. Poor word choice (Draft A-1, below), and excessive sentence length (Draft B-1, below) make sentences difficult to understand. Contrast Draft Sentences A-1 and B-1 with their final versions (A-2 and B-2).

  Draft A-1: I spent some time in Mexico where I <u>picked up some</u> Spanish.

  Final A-2: I spent some time in Mexico where I <u>polished</u> my Spanish.

  Draft B-1: While shadowing a surgeon during the summer, I watched physicians taking care of patients, talking with their families, and dealing with other health care professionals, and I finally decided that I wanted to become a surgeon so I could use my skills to help others.

  Final B-2: I decided on my future career while shadowing a surgeon during the summer. The surgeon cared for patients, calmed their families, and dealt with other health care providers. He epitomized the type of physician I want to become.

☐ 9. *Get feedback.* You have a draft in your hand. Now you need feedback to identify things to change. Run the "spell-checker" and print two double-spaced copies of your personal statement. Solicit feedback from two people. One should be a professional in the same field as the position for which you are applying. If you are applying to pharmacy school, ask a pharmacist for help. If you are applying for a physical therapy position, ask a physical therapist for her observations. The second person should be a friend or advisor who knows you very well. Ask people who will give you honest reactions. "This is great!" is not a helpful response. Ask for feedback, however, only if you are willing to listen. If all you want to hear is "That's great!" more critical comments may devastate you.

Ask the *professional* to critique your personal statement from the specialty's viewpoint. This individual should detect any obvious professional issues or problems. Should some comments be deleted? Is your personal statement complete?

When Debbie applied for a radiology technician position, she asked another technician to critique her personal statement. The reviewer suggested that she add a section describing her prior work as a laboratory technician. She did, and many of her interviewers subsequently discussed this interesting aspect of her background.

Ask your *friend* to review the document for spelling and grammatical problems. Ask if the personal statement matches your personality. Does it describe you accurately and completely? What should be added or deleted?

Emma spent a significant amount of time as a volunteer in an AIDS education project, yet she failed to state and describe how this experience affected her. Her friend asked her why she had omitted this experience from her personal statement. Emma responded that she did not know how to incorporate that experience into it. They discussed various options and finally decided to stress the fact that Emma felt very close to the high school students she taught during the project. During her visits to several pediatrics programs, some interviewers discussed this experience with her. She enjoyed talking about the project, and she emphasized the value she placed on educating and establishing rapport with patients.

Caution: Avoid asking too many people for feedback. This complicates the process and makes revisions difficult. Ask all reviewers to write their comments and suggestions. Ask them *not* to use a red pen–it's depressing!

Be prepared for opposing views. When they arise, remember that it's *your* personal statement. You must decide what to add, change, or delete. After all, it's going out with your name at the top.

Figure 9.1: First Draft of a Personal Statement With Corrections

Replace this with your name.

(Personal Statement)

Good start!
Elaborate

Medicine is the career that I've wanted to pursue since I was struck by a car when I was nine years old. I don't know *Think about and describe!* exactly why medicine interested me, but I'll always remember the way the doctors took care of me. I watched with awe as *avoid repeating phrases.* they took care of me. It was then that I decided to go to *re-write to the number of "I"s* medical school, but I changed my mind in high school after I *Say that you enjoyed courses like physics and chemistry* found that I didn't like science courses like biology.

After graduating from high school I enrolled in Central *change to their* State in (there) Civil Engineering Program. The courses were *Word choice: go with difficult* (hard) but I passed them all. I worked as an engineer for two *Good place to describe what you did!* years, but became bored with dealing just with paper and not *Emphasize problem-solving skills* people. It was then I realized that I needed other opportunities, so I decided to go back to my original career goal: Medicine. I *and completed* returned to school, took the prerequisite courses. ~~and was~~ *delete* ~~pleasantly surprised when they accepted me.~~ *stress the positive way your background helped: Taught you to set goals and maintain effort* My engineering background did not prepare me for medical *was able to* school. ~~As a result,~~ I ~~barely~~ passed all of my first year *challenged* courses. Gross Anatomy ~~was the hardest for~~ me because I have

Figure 9.1: cont'd

~~strived to understand instead of memorizing information.~~
always, ~~hated to memorize information that I'll never use.~~ I

because — state why you liked it.

liked physiology better, ~~but I had several personality conflicts~~

Avoid describing problems.

~~with some of the faculty.~~ My second year was ~~about the same~~ *more interesting*

spelling error ~~becuse~~ microbiology and pharmacology, ~~required so much~~ *exposed me to information that I knew I would use during third year.*

~~memorization.~~ Failing the USMLE Step 1 was a traumatic

Don't mention issues like these, but prepare responses in case they are raised in interviews.

experience for me, but I really didn't expect to do well because

I've always had trouble with standardized tests. ~~I finally passed~~ *delete*

~~the test after I got serious and studied.~~ I liked the clerkships

because I am a "hands-on" person. ~~Most of the year went~~ *delete*

~~smoothly expect for the problems I had with some patients and~~

~~attendings. I was recommended for "honors" in several~~

Again avoid introducing performance problems. Instead, focus on your strengths, such as analytical skills.

~~clerkships, but didn't score well enough on the exams to bet the~~

During

~~"honors" grade.~~ Medical school ~~wasn't so bad though, because~~

I ~~did~~ engage*d* in extracurricular activities such as intramural

— Did you hold any leadership positions?

sports and clubs. *specify the sports and clubs,*

I have decided to pursue a career in Family Practice. I like

Family Practice because I like to treat the entire person and *Can you be more specific?*

meet my patients' emotional and medical needs. ~~I also like~~ *These are often cited.*

delete ~~Family Practice because I think it will be easier to get a~~

This is an important paragraph. Use it to really describe positive reasons you are seeking this specialty!

Figure 9.1: cont'd

delete

~~residency position since there are a lot of Family Practice~~

~~residency programs.~~

☺ Great Start!

Outside of medicine I like to play golf, tennis, and

Describe how you became such a good golfer — e.g., discipline, practice, etc.

basketball. My friends say that I'm a great golfer and should be on the professional tour. [In fact, my game has improved so much during medical school that I hope to eventually turn pro after finishing my residency program.]

Consider deleting this sentence— Unless many of the key people are golfers.

Too general. This describes 99.94% of all med students!

~~I am disciplined, work hard, and have a positive attitude.~~ I ~~am~~ really excited about the possibility of joining the residency program at St. Paul's Medical Center. I've heard many good things about the program, and I know that its the kind of

↳ it's

program that I can be happy and productive in. I am available

for an interview at you're convenience.

↳ your

Don't "play up to" a program. People are wise to those who can insert a name/institution with great ease using a computer.

No, No!

Describe what you want in your residency program. Diverse patient population (mention your languages, like Spanish)? Teaching opportunities? Research opportunities? Rural or urban setting? etc.

* Overall, <u>a good start</u>. Now revise and emphasize your strengths!

☐ 10. *Revise as needed.* Revising a draft is like polishing a stone. It takes effort and time, but the results are worth all the trouble. Rename your computer file with each revision (PS01.DOC, PS02.DOC or PSJan02.001, PSJan5.005) so you can keep track of the current revision. Keep the prior versions until you have finished the final version. At some point, though, you will have to declare it done. (For hints on naming files, see Chapter 4.)

☐ 11. *Check the final copy for grammatical and spelling errors.* You and a friend should check the final draft for grammatical and spelling errors. *Do not* rely completely on a computer spell-checker because "their is two many ways a error can be maid" and the program could miss them (as this sentence illustrates).

☐ 12. *Print it on a laser or ink-jet printer and send it.* Do not use a dot-matrix printer. Even the best dot-matrix printers do not look professional. Print it on the same color and weight of paper as your résumé. Don't fold your personal statement. Place it in a large envelope that will hold the statement without having to fold it. Then mail it. It will never be perfect, but it must be received to be read.

☐ 13. *Repeat the process as necessary.* If you apply to more than one program or to multiple employers, try to individualize your personal statement for each. Are some of the potential readers looking for different attributes? If so, a generic personal statement will not be optimal. Individualize the paragraphs about yourself to highlight the different skills and traits being sought.

10: Health Professionals' Personal Statements: Examples

A personal statement should reflect you and your personality.

Actual personal statements

This chapter contains actual personal statements. They illustrate how different people have inventoried their marketable strengths and, each in his own way, distilled those qualities onto one page. Although many of these examples were used to apply to medical school or residency programs, the styles are similar to those that any health professional (or prospective health professional) will use.

The authors are real people. I worked with many of them as they wrote their personal statements. Their personal statements describe, directly and indirectly, each person's individual and professional development.

As you review these personal statements, notice if you "connect" with the writer. What do you like about each personal statement? What stands out in your mind after reading each document? What experiences or attributes do you share with the author?

I hope you enjoy these personal statements as much as I do. I can visualize the authors as I read their statements. I appreciate the writers' allowing me to use their documents to help you in the process of writing your personal statement. These documents are printed essentially as they were mailed. The name and some personal material within each statement have been changed however, to protect the guilty. You see what the selection committees saw. As you read, try to visualize their faces. I know you'll like them as much as I. Enjoy!

List of personal statements

Name	Position applying for:
1. E. Allen Poe	Master of Public Health
2. Michael Sorongopong	Medical school
3. Helene S. Seyler	Medical school
4. Phoebe B. Weidner	Medical school
5. Mary Shelly	Medical school
6. P.S. "Mike" Nguyen	Medical school
7. Katherine Ann Porter	Medical school (Older applicant)
8. Mary Lou McKean	Medical Technology school
9. Thomas X. Mathias	Paramedic school
10. David L. Soren	Physical Therapy school
11. Thomas S. Harlan	Physician Assistant program
12. Nicholas A. Nekrasov	Anesthesia residency
13. Alicia Thompson	Anesthesia residency
14. Pablo Cassals	Emergency Medicine residency
15. Frederick Pascal	Emergency Medicine residency
16. Maria Lopez	Family Practice residency
17. Susan Ellerbee	Internal Medicine residency
18. Stanley Lu	Internal Medicine residency
19. Lawrence I. Stanley	Internal Medicine residency
20. Andrew R. Jackson	Neurology residency
21. Phillipe Ariés	Preventive Medicine/Rehab. residency (FMG)
22. Assad L. Sayah	Radiation Oncology residency (IMG)
23. Mark Anthony	Radiology residency
24. Julie Wang	Surgery residency
25. Albert Jonson	Cardiology fellowship
26. Florence Nightingale	Nurse Practitioner
27. Robert J. Openheimer, M.D.	Physician-changing specialty
28. Gertrude Stein, M.D.	Physician-changing specialty

E. Allen Poe

I first selected a career in medicine because I wanted to help people and have a challenging profession. My undergraduate experiences reinforced this decision. Tutoring undergraduate students in chemistry and serving as president of our university's pre-medical organization helped me develop communication and leadership skills. Participating in the honors program taught me debating and team-building skills that I can use in the future. Maintaining an active lifestyle has helped me to understand the importance of a healthy body and to appreciate the concerns of people who are ill or injured.

During medical school, two extracurricular activities exposed me to the limits of one-to-one patient-physician interactions. The first was working in a student-run clinic for medically underserved children. At the clinic I saw children with many diverse health care needs. I realized that the solutions to their needs extended far beyond the capabilities provided by one-to-one physician contacts. I saw this with more intensity as I assumed increasing levels of responsibility and came to know the children and their parents personally. The second was my involvement with the American Medical Student Association (AMSA). AMSA also gave me a broader view of health care issues. I coordinated a regional conference "Serving the Underserved Children at Home and Abroad," and met numerous physicians who worked with underserved children. The conference included a trip to Mexico, where we visited a squatters' settlement, saw crowded day-care facilities, and toured health care clinics. Interacting with these individuals showed me that physicians who care for underserved children must be involved with community issues.

Thus, during my second year of medical school, I had an excellent exposure to public health. It was then that I decided to include public health in my career plans. The main reason for this decision is my desire to increase the impact I have on people's needs. Furthermore, I like the interdisciplinary approach of public health; I enjoy collaborating with people from different professional backgrounds and interests. I also want to teach so that I can motivate others to become involved with public health issues. Finally, I want to impact public health policy through research and activism. I realize that my current education is limited, and that I need further training in epidemiology, statistics, and other public health disciplines. My ultimate career plans are to balance clinical practice in a primary care specialty with research, activism, and leadership in the public health domain.

I want to pursue the Master of Public Health Program with a concentration in Public Management and Children's Health. I chose this concentration primarily because I am interested in directing efforts to improve children's health on many levels. I seek a public health program that can help me learn the concepts necessary to research ways to better provide health care services to children and to implement these means. After completing this program, I will enter a residency in Public Health and Preventive Medicine.

On a personal level, my favorite activities are bicycling, running, knitting, and modern dance. I enjoy all outdoor sports, and I like group activities. My family lives in Cleveland, Ohio and is a source of support for me.

145

Michael Sorongopong

"You'll never get into medical school!" said my so-called pre-med advisor (a professor of chemistry) during my sophomore year in college. "Why?" I asked. "Because you just don't have it. No education major will ever be dressed in surgical scrubs–except at Halloween," he said. "Thanks a lot," I replied. That's the last time I saw this "advisor." Despite this temporary ego deflation, I pursued my own dream–to be a physician-educator.

To that end, I will be getting a degree in secondary education with specialization in biology and general science education. Rather than fulfilling only the basic requirements for the degree, however, I selected the more rigorous science courses from the pre-medical curriculum. Now I have not only a science, but also a formal educational methodology background to bring to my career in medicine. This path broadened my horizons far beyond those of many of my colleagues. I have student-taught in an inner-city school, actually learned to use (and in many cases produce) the audiovisual aids and equipment necessary for many presentations, and polished my public speaking skills and ability to instruct others. I acquired these skills among aspiring educators, whose goal is to positively influence our next generation. I don't believe that there could be a better setting for someone planning a career in medicine.

Sometimes, however, my reach exceeded my grasp. I took Embryology during the spring of my sophomore year. "Why not?" I thought. Only when I got into the course did I realize that pre-med "hard-science" majors only took it in their last semester, so their grade would appear only after they already had their acceptance from medical school. It was that tough. Why did I get a "C" in the course? Truthfully, I worked like a dog for it. I'm very proud of that grade.

My spare time revolves around three centers: my fraternity, Alpha Phi Omega (the national service fraternity), the local volunteer fire department, and my fiancée. Our fraternity not only helps students on our campus in many ways, but it also raises large amounts of money for charities (particularly Muscular Dystrophy). We also, of course, have social activities to keep us going. The fire department takes up one complete day each weekend (24 hours). I am a state-certified Fire Fighter and EMT, and due to our high activity level, I get to use both skills frequently. Last, but certainly not least, is my beautiful fiancée. She has consistently supported my goals and is currently finishing her own degree in accounting.

Education is my life and medicine will be my life. Combining these two should prove to be a powerful and dynamic package. How short-sighted that pre-med advisor was.

HELENE S. SEYLER

For the past six years I have worked in the Cardiothoracic Intensive Care Unit of our busy tertiary care teaching hospital, first as a staff nurse and then as head nurse. And, for the past six years, not a week has passed when a physician didn't ask me why I wasn't practicing medicine. In the early years I answered, correctly, that I *was* practicing medicine, as a nurse. Yet I began thinking how much more I could accomplish as a physician. Now I answer that I am practicing medicine as a nurse and soon will practice medicine as a caring *and* curing physician.

The pre-med road hasn't been easy for me, however. Although I had a B.S.N., my science courses were rudimentary compared to those taken by the pre-med students at our university. I struggled mightily through the advanced chemistry, biology, and physics classes. As you may infer from my transcript, the calculus course almost killed me, but I stuck it out and passed. Just taking the courses was difficult, since I was working full-time, often on swing or night shifts. The only times I could study at work were on my half-hour "lunch" breaks or when few patients were sick enough to warrant coming to our unit. (That happened only on two of my shifts in the past six years.) Even though many of my fellow students marveled at how I could go to school and hold down a job, I had, in a way, an easier time than they did. I knew exactly why I wanted to go to medical school, was "intensively" involved in delivering health care, and had the "big picture" of what I was getting into. My resolve was firm, even through the adversity.

Even though it seems as if I shouldn't have had any spare time, my philosophy is that you have time for what is important to you. I manage to squeeze in a daily swim (a holdover from my days as a high school competitive swimmer), and to go hiking with friends. I also collect U.S. stamps, a hobby I picked up as a child and that I find both intellectually stimulating and relaxing.

Given my background, I expect that I will look at all of the critical care specialties very carefully when I decide on a field of medicine to enter. Yet, I know that I have not seen many of the other faces of medicine, so my career may take another direction. No matter what course I pursue, however, I will take with me, and expand on, the wonderful experiences I have already had as an ICU nurse.

Phoebe B. Weidner

Working with Marcus Welby, M.D., brought me to a career in medicine. Not that I really worked with this fictional television doctor, but I did even better—I worked with the real-life equivalent. His name is Dr. Louis Olson, and as a Family Practitioner, he took care of me and my family as I was growing up. Later, I worked for him as an office assistant while I was in high school and college. The caring and idealism I saw exemplified the best in humanity. He is the complete physician, not only seeing patients in the office and at the hospital, but also making frequent house calls to homebound patients. Knowing my interest in medicine, he occasionally let me accompany him on these visits. I want to follow in his footsteps.

My background is a bit unusual, but even that now seems the norm. The most unusual part is that I come from a stable, caring home. Nevertheless, I did the foolish thing of getting married right out of high school and immediately having a beautiful child, Sarah. I quickly became a single mother (through divorce), I continued in school, however, thanks to the help of my family. Even though I went to school full-time, worked part-time, and took care of Sarah, my grades were surprisingly good. I learned to nurse her while studying—quite a feat of dexterity and concentration. The only area I fell down in was my MCAT scores. I can only say that my deep involvement in medicine contributed to the poor performance. (I was in the emergency room the entire night before the exam with Sarah. Thank you, she's doing fine now.)

My future course in medicine is purposely cloudy. I know that the scope of medical practice is wide, and I don't want to limit myself without seeing all of the options available. I am, however, continually drawn back to my image of Dr. Olson sitting at the bedside of an elderly woman with terminal cancer. He held her hand and said, "I'll be sure you aren't in pain." Being that type of doctor is my goal.

Mary Shelly

Many nursery rhymes were written to hide their political statements. "Humpty Dumpty," for example, slyly commented on British politics. As a child of four, however, it wasn't the politics that disturbed me, but rather, what did "all the King's horses and all the King's men" know about medicine? Poor Humpty had a medical emergency and there was no real help in sight. That is my first remembered thought about medicine.

How was it that a child of four thought about the medical aspects of this common nursery rhyme? Growing up, I was surrounded by medicine. My grandfather, uncle, and father were doctors. My mother is a clinical psychologist, and many of the adults who visited our home were doctors. Medicine, while not an explicit part of most conversations, was, nevertheless, a pervasive undercurrent.

My first ventures into practicing medicine were with animals. With my parent's forbearance, I supervised the care of all types of wild "critters" that came my way. My family, of course, helped me out. But for these animals, I was their "doctor," and I loved it. In retrospect, I'm surprised how many lived and were returned to the wild.

Veterinary medicine, however, is not for me. I gave it a short trial as a veterinary assistant during high school. It soon became apparent that my calling was in human medicine. To that end, I have volunteered in hospitals (wards, pediatrics, emergency departments), worked as an office/laboratory assistant in my uncle's primary care office, and served as a volunteer first aider on our college's volunteer ambulance.

What I have confirmed is that medicine remains my calling. I plan to put the Humpty Dumptys of the world back together again. I will not only be good at doing it, but I will also love every minute of it.

Mary Shelly

P.S. "Mike" Nguyen

The Vietnam War affected different people in different ways. For me it was a way of life, being born in Saigon. Fortunately for me, my parents supplied me with an excellent French-Vietnamese education until the age of fourteen, when the northern communists overthrew our government and took over Saigon. In the midst of this anarchy, the new government ordered a beautification project for the city to celebrate the victory. Students did the work. It changed my life.

Divided into groups of five, we worked to clean up the streets littered with garbage, Southern Army uniforms, dead animals, and human bodies. Suddenly, an explosion ripped the air in an alley a few feet from me. Turning the corner, I found three of my friends lying on the ground, each in his own pool of blood from a thousand pieces of metal. S. died instantly when the grenades fell from the khaki trousers he had picked up. T. and P. gasped for air not far from S.'s warm corpse. Instead of coming to our rescue, bystanders did the opposite; they fled from the unknown, responsibility, and another possible explosion. T. and P. died soon afterwards, with P. mumbling incoherently before dying in my arms. It was not that I hadn't seen death before, but even with my Boy Scout first aid, that brought home the true meaning of helplessness.

My family escaped from Vietnam three years later, arriving in Washington, D.C., where I attended high school. I then entered the University of Maryland on a full academic scholarship. I majored in Biology and received multiple academic awards, despite working as a grocery store checker/bag-boy to financially assist my family. I graduated *Summa Cum Laude* and was immediately recruited by a high-tech genetics engineering firm, where I have received multiple promotions. My dream of helping others, however, would not die.

With my family's support, I now plan to move on to my life's calling–practicing medicine. My personal motivations include not only my need to help others, but also my need to fill the void of my boyhood comrades who would have contributed so much to society. That is my goal.

Katherine Anne Porter

Why would I, a 46-year-old woman, be willing to invest the time and energy it takes to become a physician? The answer is simple: Becoming a physician is an extension of my eleven-year commitment to medicine.

I was reared on a homestead in the Alaskan woods after the Second World War. The nearest doctors were over 100-miles away, or on the hospital ships that came to Alaska for the Public Health Department. A nurse who lived in our settlement acted as the local doctor out of necessity. Despite this limited exposure to medicine, I knew that I wanted a career in medicine. After relocating to Michigan, I attended St. Michael's School of Nursing in Detroit.

I began work as a Pediatric staff nurse at St. Michael's Hospital in Detroit. Within six months I was promoted to head nurse of that same Pediatric Department. After working there for a year I returned home to Alaska, where I worked in a clinic during the day while by night I was "on call" for maternity patients. Our community didn't have a hospital until 1970, and the clinic functioned as the hospital for maternity and emergency patients.

After marrying, I moved to Portland, Oregon. Initially I worked at Johnstown Medical Center in Portland as the chief pediatric nurse. A year later we moved to Concord, California so that my husband could continue his education. There I worked at Concord's Children's Hospital for four years as the charge nurse of a large Cardiovascular Surgical–Neonatal ICU before becoming the evening shift supervisor. As head nurse in the ICU, I functioned as the "Code Nurse" on my shift for the entire hospital until doctors could arrive.

In 1975, I began working as the charge nurse of the Medical–Coronary ICU at Duke University Medical Center. A year later the medical director asked me to fill the position of Clinical Nurse Specialist in Cardiology. In that capacity, I ran the Anticoagulation Clinic, the Pacemaker Clinic, supervised all the exercise treadmill tests, and saw patients in the Cardiology Clinic. During the five years I worked as a Nurse Specialist in Cardiology, I published six articles with the program's physicians.

I divorced my husband in 1979 and remarried in 1982. I left my position at the Medical Center and became a full-time wife, and a mother to my two children and two step-children. When they were all in school I had some free time during the day. Thus began my second career–volunteerism. For the last ten years I have helped raise millions of dollars for the children of Durham through Children's Charities, Inc. I have also raised money for the American Heart Association, the Medical Center's Children's Research Unit, and the Heart Center. Currently I am on the Boards of Directors of Children's Charities, Inc., and the Medical Center's Heart Unit.

Why didn't I pursue medical school earlier? In 1965, my advanced algebra teacher told me I was incapable of doing algebra and that I should not take any more math. In the early 1960s little was known about dyslexia, so my diagnosis was left until I was 43-years old and taking chemistry. In all my years of nursing I never encountered any problems as a result of my dyslexia. I could read charts, understand doctor's orders, written or verbal, and administer medications. I functioned competently and confidently despite the dyslexia.

An obvious question is, given my age, will the length of my medical practice justify my investment in medical education? The answer lies in my commitment to medicine. I intend to practice as long as I am physically able. Current mortality rates suggest that I can reasonably expect to live beyond seventy-eight years of age. This suggests a practice of 20+ years.

A good physician accepts the responsibility for the welfare of the patient and is willing to make decisions that are at times very difficult. After working as a nurse and Clinical Nurse Specialist, I know that I have the ability to be an excellent physician. I have the desire and the ability to communicate with people, to understand their worries, and to deliver excellent patient care.

Mary Lou McKean

❖❖❖

Working with chemicals and in laboratories has always fascinated me. The idea of doing this and getting paid for it too, seems like an extraordinary opportunity. That is why I am applying for acceptance to the School of Medical Technology.

Currently, I am completing my sophomore year at Missouri State University with a major in chemistry. I do not, however, want either a career in chemistry or to go on for a Ph.D. What I really want to do is to apply this information in a laboratory setting. It is in the laboratory, following protocols and doing tests that I am the happiest. After investigating several options, including discussing the positive and negative aspects of the field with several clinical and research medical technologists, I believe that medical technology is the route for me. Even what they consider the negative aspects of their jobs, such as repeatedly running many of the same tests, does not take the luster off the field. There is, of course, the additional bonus of actually helping sick people by running the tests accurately and quickly.

I have been very busy as an undergraduate student. In addition to my studies, I compete actively in intercollegiate volleyball, work part-time for a local veterinarian (often running laboratory tests), and tutor high school students in chemistry.

I see my work as a medical technologist probably being in a small hospital, large clinic, or on the night shift, where I can be a "jack-of-all-trades," doing tests normally assigned to only one lab in a large hospital. This will fit in well with my personality and allow me to maximally use my med tech education to its fullest. Eventually, I may move on to a research lab where I can participate in developing new tests. But, as they say, that is for the future. Now, I just can't wait to get started.

❖❖❖

THOMAS X. MATHIAS

For the past six months I have been enormously frustrated! During this time, I worked full time as an EMT on our rural ambulance. The closest hospital for treatment of anything serious is 60 to 90 minutes away by ground, and serious injuries only seem to happen when the helicopters are grounded for weather or maintenance or are already on flights. Our patients, *my patients*, need paramedic-level services. I am the right person to begin providing this service.

I grew up in rural Patchel County, working on a dairy farm. I went to school and married here, and have multiple ties to our community. I left for a year to attend college, but although I did well, I felt lost so far from my home and family. Upon returning, I not only got reacquainted with farm work, but also joined the volunteer fire department. Soon after that, at the urging of the fire chief, I began taking the course for Emergency Medical Technician certification. I became the sixth member of our department to certify as an EMT, and the third EMT to work full-time for the department.

Over the past six months, our ambulance calls have accelerated dramatically, going from about six per week to about four per day. In part, that is due to the rapid population increase (suburbanization) in our area, as well as better access to the 911 system. What we all now realize is that we need to significantly upgrade our ambulance service. With this in mind, and with the full support of the fire chief, I am applying for paramedic training. As you know, Riverside Medical Center has already agreed to act as my base station when I successfully complete the course.

My long term goal is to not only complete paramedic school myself, but also to help staff our county's ambulance service with full-time paramedics. I will do this either by recruiting other members of our department to take the training or by hiring paramedics who have completed training. This is neither a long-term nor a futile objective. I have the support of both the fire chief and the community for this effort. If we delay, we will only be playing catch-up. Our community deserves better than that.

David L. Soren

When I woke up in the hospital, my first though was definitely not about physical therapy. Rather, it was what in the heck am I doing here? Slowly, I began to remember my end-of-the-day attempt at skiing the "black diamond" route. When I tried to move my right arm and leg I started to figure out what had happened. Not only hadn't I made it, but my body was a mess. My arm was in a cast (with multiple pins sticking out) and my leg was in traction. (They wouldn't pin my leg for several more days.) Later I found out I had also been on a ventilator for the first twenty-four hours after the accident–having had a close encounter with a tree. I was lucky to be alive.

My awareness of physical therapy came later, when a cute young thing (now my wife) came to the bedside to assess my needs for physical therapy. It turned out she was a student. What I didn't know was she also had an enormous amount of knowledge about the musculoskeletal system, steel hands to help me move, and an iron will to help me get back into shape. Wow, was I impressed.

As I gradually met other members of the Physical Therapy department, I learned that she was not unique (in her physical therapy skills or knowledge). The whole department was filled with professional, motivated people pursuing a career that genuinely helped patients. Among my fellow patients, I saw some who thought they would never walk or live independently again surpass their wildest dreams with the help of the PTs. It dawned on me that physical therapy was what I was meant to do.

Of course, as a pseudo-athlete I was always peripherally aware of physical therapists, trainers, and similar folks. But they were for the "real jocks." Now I know how pervasive their job really is, and I want to be part of it.

At present, I am completing the prerequisite courses for physical therapy school, having completed my B.A. in Anthropology two years ago. I look forward to beginning my PT education with the goal of following in my own, almost disastrous, "ski-steps" by working primarily in sports medicine. Hopefully I will do for others what my wife did for me.

Thomas S. Harlan, P.A.

Physician Assistant school, going to college, and my military career stand out as my life's major achievements. Coming from a town in rural Kentucky where no one had ever finished college, one of my earliest life goals was to not only to go to college, but to get a degree. With the help of a military scholarship, I succeeded. This, however, only started the adventure.

Following college, I entered the military (second lieutenant) in the Medical Service Corps (hospital/clinic management). While my work was interesting, I found myself constantly gravitating to patient care areas, watching the clinicians in action. That seemed really exciting, but I did not see a way for me to get into it. Nursing seemed a bit tame and medical school was out-of-reach, at least until I finished my service commitment. Suddenly, however, a notice came across my desk that Medical Service Corps officers could now apply to Physician Assistant school. (They had previously not been readily accepted.) This was my chance, and I took it. I sent in my own application before day's end–and I got in.

The next two years were a blur of activity, as I first did the intensive classroom work and then the year of "clinicals." After graduating, my initial assignment was to the hospital where I had done my clinicals. There I worked in the primary care clinic, seeing my own panel of patients. Soon, however, I was assigned to an independent duty post. This put me in a clinic about three hours away from any other health care professional. Not only did I administratively run the clinic and supervise the fifteen corpsman (my Medical Service Corps duties came in handy here), but I was also responsible for the health of all of the military personnel and their families in the area. A physician came once a week to see consults, review my records, and give me a chance to "talk medicine." I was overstressed, I was overworked, I was overjoyed. It was great!

After serving two tours at that post, I reluctantly returned to teach at the military's PA school. While important, this duty took me away from my primary love, seeing patients. Therefore, I have decided to leave the military and once again tend to patient care. My fine training and independent duty experience have optimally prepared me to work in rural or remote areas, with a diverse population, and to provide excellent patient care.

Nicholas A. Nekrasov

I was first exposed to anesthesiology two years before entering medical school, while working towards a Ph.D. in Electrical Engineering. As I designed a system to measure the effects of anesthetic agents on isolated myocardial contractility, the highly technical nature of the equipment and the complexities of patient monitoring intrigued me. Although I maintained an active interest in other clinical specialties as I progressed through my clinical rotations during medical school, I felt increasingly certain that anesthesiology could best utilize my creative research and technical skills. My anesthesiology rotation solidified this impression.

A career in anesthesiology will permit me to combine my interest in direct patient care with my engineering training. By stimulating my fascination with both medicine and engineering, anesthesiology will allow me to participate in patient contacts and to explore applied physiology and pharmacology. I enjoy performing procedures, experiencing the intense atmosphere in the operating room, and working with committed and personable physicians who assume a variety of responsibilities.

While pursuing an M.D. and a Ph.D., I was the principal investigator for numerous research and design projects. These led to the development of several medical devices–including the automated system to dynamically measure the effects of anesthetic agents on myocardial contractility in isolated tissue preparations, an ambulatory computerized multichannel muscle stimulator/TENS unit, and a computerized radiofrequency ablation controller. My graduate engineering work will culminate in a dissertation, *A thermodynamic model of radiofrequency catheter ablation for the treatment of cardiac arrhythmias*, outlining the mathematical modeling of radiofrequency catheter ablation of cardiac tissue. I was responsible not only for developing a research design, but also for obtaining funding for all of my postgraduate work.

I have balanced my academic, clinical, and research responsibilities with an active personal life. I have been married for four years to a wonderfully supportive dentist who understands the demands of a medical career. She encourages me intellectually and spiritually. In my spare time, I love to run, cycle, and swim, and my wife and I can think of nothing better than spending a weekend snow skiing. I also enjoy restoring classic automobiles. At the moment, I am reconstructing a 1966 Mustang from the ground up. Finally, I build audio equipment, particularly high-end audio amplifiers.

My goal is to enter a research-oriented anesthesiology residency program. First and foremost, I wish to learn the fundamentals, expanding my skills and building a solid foundation for my future practice of anesthesiology. However, I want to continue participating in research projects during my residency. Ultimately, I would like a joint appointment in anesthesiology and engineering at a respected research institution. In essence, much of my research, though technically centered, aims to improve the quality of care–if the devices are more accurate, and the diagnostic tests more precise, we can replace some of our uncertainties with expeditious treatment, backing up compassion with results.

Alicia Thompson

Working as a dietitian prior to entering medical school, I found myself most interested in enteral and parenteral nutrition, due to the nature of nutrition support delivery. I was intrigued by the physiologic response to stress, disease, and medical treatment. Observing the results of certain drug therapies and treatments made me wonder how they worked. At St. Michael's Hospital, I worked closely with physicians and this, combined with my curiosity to know the mechanism of action of drugs and the rationale for various treatments, stimulated me to broaden my horizons.

Medical school has been a challenging and enjoyable experience. During the two years of basic sciences, my favorite subjects were Pharmacology and Physiology. The interaction of the processes of human physiology fascinated me; in Pharmacology, I was intrigued by the manipulation and exploitation of normal physiologic processes to allow healing, normalization of function, and relief of pain. My transition to third-year clinical clerkships was a smooth one, which I credit to a strong knowledge base and my prior health care experience. Contact with patients, their families, and members of the health care team have reminded me of the importance of interpersonal skills, as well as underscoring my enjoyment of these interactions. I have been stimulated to learn by the excitement of applying knowledge gained in the first two years to clinical situations. I have been fortunate to work with physicians who challenged me to achieve my fullest potential and as a result, earned honors evaluations in all my third-year clerkships.

I am pursuing residency training and a career in anesthesiology. During my clerkships in anesthesiology, I enjoyed the intellectual stimulation and opportunity to apply my knowledge of pharmacology to predict and observe immediate physiologic responses to drugs. Additionally, I was able to help patients both physically and emotionally during acute pain, chronic pain, and the perioperative period. I like using my hands to perform associated procedures, such as intubating and placing arterial and central lines.

I will make an excellent anesthesiologist for several reasons. First, I possess a strong information base and the desire to further my knowledge. Second, I am a logical thinker who can solve complex clinical problems quickly. Third, I am a "team player" who enjoys working with others to achieve the optimal result for the patient. I am creative and flexible in planning strategies to reach the goals of patient care and, while I take direction well, I can convey my thoughts and assume leadership in appropriate situations. My prior work experience and part-time employment during medical school have emphasized the importance of goal setting, prioritization, and delegation. Fourth, I have excellent listening skills. This has helped me deal with families and patients stressed by illness or surgery, as well as with physicians and other health care professionals. Fifth, I am a competent educator and see teaching as a means to increase someone else's knowledge while adding to my own. Finally, outside interests and a sense of humor allow me to keep a balance in my own life and increase my enthusiasm for medical practice.

I look forward to a career in anesthesiology involving clinical practice, research, and education. During my own medical education, I have become increasingly aware of the importance of research and will seek out opportunities to participate in anesthesiology research. I find teaching a gratifying and stimulating aspect of practice that can be assimilated into almost any situation. My knowledge of clinical medicine will be enhanced by my knowledge of dietetics, business, and education to make me a valuable member in the field of anesthesiology. I seek a program that will help me to achieve my career goals.

Pablo Cassals ———————————————————

I stand before the double doors of the emergency department, remembering my prior experiences. I knew the ED as a student and wonder if it will look different to me as a doctor. Through these doors today will pass a motor vehicle accident victim, a toothache, a cardiac arrest, and a child with undiagnosed leukemia. Will I be up to the task of helping these people?

I remember the awe I felt as a medical student the first time I stepped through these same doors through which 90,000 patients per year would pass. I was confident, unduly and brashly confident, that I could organize and arrange priorities, treat simple and even some life-threatening problems, and generally do well in this environment. This confidence was based on my years as a paramedic. The skills were there. I just didn't know how much I had yet to learn.

I look at these doors, holding back the serenity of the world outside and smile, remembering the seeming confusion, even mayhem within their portals. The bleeding patient screaming in Spanish to a physician who could not understand her cries. Her husband, threatening the physician with a demeanor that transcended language barriers. My first ED patient encounter was to interpret for that patient and get her needs met.

I think of the cardiac patient who came in with an unusual atrial arrhythmia. My exposure to cardiac research and experience with EKGs allowed me to suggest the appropriate diagnosis and treatment to the supervising resident, who appreciated the help. Later I did my first unsupervised cutdown on a trauma patient. My line infused; the patient died. Overall, a mixed experience.

As I stand here, an emergency physician walks wearily through the opening doors, reminding me of how grueling this work can be. I know, however, that my commitment to the specialty is strong, based as it is on several years of paramedic experience, not just student rotations. I believe I can weather both the mental and physical challenges of the specialty, and that my avocations of weightlifting and long-distance running will give me the stamina for the common 12-hour-long shifts.

As I prepare to walk through these ED doors again, I mostly feel a sense of exhilaration that I will be part of this, the most basic and intense of all medical experiences: saving lives, comforting the distressed, relieving pain, and providing health care to those who have nowhere else to turn.

FREDERICK PASCAL

My interest in Emergency Medicine began while I was in high school. I completed an EMT course during the summer before I started college. While in the emergency department, I observed physicians caring for patients, interacting with their families, and directing pre-hospital care. I decided that I wanted to become an Emergency Physician. I worked as a hospital orderly while also volunteering in the emergency department until the end of my second year of college. At that time, I was offered a position as an Orthopedic and Emergency Technician. These experiences further motivated me, reinforcing my desire to attend medical school.

While in medical school I have been involved with the Homeless Shelter Clinic (HSC) and the Emergency Medical Services students' club. The Shelter's clinic gave me hands-on patient care experience during my pre-clinical years. The emergency medicine club helped me to develop administrative skills through writing articles for the newsletter, and organizing meetings and scheduling the speakers. In addition, I arranged for active club members to take ACLS courses at no charge.

During my third year I completed rotations not only at the University hospital, but also at the Evergreen Medical Center, Brooke Army Medical Center, the Dallas VA Hospital, and a local community health center. These experiences exposed me to a wide range of hospital styles and sizes, and to differing patient populations. I also spent time in the busy ED of a hospital adjacent to the state school for the deaf, where I acquired a basic knowledge of American Sign Language.

My long-standing interest in Emergency Medical Services persists. Emergency Medicine's fast pace, community involvement, and the required broad knowledge base continue to attract me. The Emergency Medical system comes together to help all people. I want to be an active part of that system.

I wish to enter a residency program that will provide a broad-based clinical education with a diverse patient population. During my residency training, I want to teach hospital and pre-hospital personnel, pursue research, and be involved in Emergency Medical Services. I seek a program that emphasizes education, encourages mentoring, and provides feedback on my performance.

Both of my parents emigrated from Northern Africa. Their international experiences have encouraged me to travel. In 1985, I spent the summer near Marseilles in the south of France, learning French. The following summer I backpacked through England and Scotland for a few weeks, visiting many of the places where my parents grew up. I have also traveled through much of the western United States, and Canada and Mexico. In addition to traveling, I enjoy hiking, skiing and scuba diving. The knowledge that I have gained while working in the ED and at medical school has added a new dimension to these endeavors. I am particularly interested in wilderness and environmental emergencies, and in international health.

One Doctor's Life

A Personal Script by Maria Lopez

Scene I: The Interview

Cast of Characters:

- **Maria Lopez:** a 31-year-old female who is unique and creative, yet practical. She has the ability to adapt to many situations and also challenges the boundaries with imagination and humor. She believes in herself and is a solid worker who is reliable, competent, and proud. All of these qualities are covered with a humble and endearing aura.

- **The Interviewer:** male or female, this character is not identifiable by gender but by authority and wisdom. An individual with a rich history of trials and tribulations, who possesses the qualities of fairness and justice, and who can also appreciate warmth and beauty.

Place: Hospital We-Care, Anytown, U.S.A.
Time: 10:50 a.m., one weekday

Lights come up on the Interviewer's office which has an eclectic decor. Books, journals, and papers are piled on the floor, table, chair, and bookcase. Knickknacks from foreign adventures fill up any other space available. The Interviewer is swearing and muttering curses under her breath. A knock is heard at the door.

INT: [*shouting*] Come in! [*another knock is heard*] Come in! Be quick about it!

ML: [*popping her head in around the door*] Excuse me, but did you say come in?

INT: Yes, yes come in. Do me a favor will you? Start looking for a blue folder that says "Grand Rounds" on it. I'm giving a presentation in 10 minutes, and I haven't even found my slides yet!

ML: [*rolling up her sleeves and plunging into a pile*] Grand Rounds Lecture? Bummer. I guess there's some sort of mix-up. Your secretary has us scheduled for an interview at 11 o'clock.

INT: [*stops and turns to look at Lopez*] Don't tell me. You're the med student who wants to go into Family Practice.

ML: [*nodding her head vigorously and sticking out her hand to shake while simultaneously trying to hold on to a large pile of papers*] That's me, Maria Lopez and very pleased to meet you.

INT: [*throwing down a stack of journals in disgust*] God! I hate it when this happens! I'm sorry, but I told my secretary to reschedule us for later. Grand Rounds was sprung on me two days ago. [*reaching for her schedule book*] Let's see, what does one o'clock look like for you?

160

ML: Uh...about 12,000 feet. [*the Interviewer looks at her with puzzlement*] I mean my flight back to Michigan leaves at 12:45 p.m., and I'm guessing that's where I'll be–12,000 feet up. By the way, is this what you're looking for? [*hands interviewer a blue folder*]

INT: Ah, excellent! [*looks at contents then back at Lopez*] Okay, let's cut straight to the point then. You have two minutes. Tell me why you want to go into Family Practice.

ML: [*placing the papers on the chair*] I believe Family Practice will allow me to experience the great variety of pathology that afflicts the human being as a whole. [*lights fade and a spotlight frames her*] I will be able to work with the spectrum of ages and appreciate their particular needs, from Pediatrics to Geriatrics. [*music begins*] I'll portray the roles of counselor, teacher, leader and friend, and I'll be able to handle common everyday problems whether it be Aunt Ida's ingrown toenail or Uncle Harry's hypertension. [*spotlight widens to include a waving American flag in background*] But mostly, Family Practice allows for geographical freedom. The fact that I could be useful in rural settings, suburbs, or inner cities is the biggest attraction for me. When I enter Family Practice I hope to work with a group of professionals who function as a team. I hope that they are open-minded and receptive to new techniques and approaches, and combine these with the more traditional methods for the benefit of the patient. [*music fades, lights come up and there is silence*]

NIT: [*staring at Lopez–her features say nothing*] And the real reason?

ML: [*at first surprised, but then shrugs her shoulders*] Because... *I like it.*

NIT: Great! Help me with this projector, Lopez, and walk with me to the auditorium. I want to introduce you to some important people, and to recommend you for our match.

ML: [*grabbing the projector and holding the door open in a smooth and elegant motion*] Thanks! I appreciate that.

NIT: Know any good jokes I can use to begin my presentation? [*steps out the door with Lopez following and lights begin to fade*]

ML: You could ask them what they'd get if a Cabbage Patch™ Doll is mixed with the Pillsbury® Doughboy. [*lights continue to fade, there is silence for a few seconds and then a big hearty laugh is heard from far away*] [*Black out*]

Susan Ellerbe

The sun sets on the horizon near San Diego as I come to the end of a long, solitary walk. The ocean winds cool me as I reflect on the past and how I developed into the person I am today.

I was born and grew up in San Diego–seemingly with a stethoscope around my neck. When someone asked what I wanted to be when I grew up, I unhesitatingly replied, "a physician." During high school I participated in numerous service activities including two years in Amigos de Las Americas, an organization whose members spend summers in Central America administering various health programs. I taught dental hygiene in rural areas of the Dominican Republic and administered vaccinations in urban Mexico. The experience and empathy I gained still influence me today.

In college I continued along the path towards becoming a physician. I worked at Concord Medical Center and was involved in many on- and off-campus activities. Looking back, it is difficult to discern exactly when I set my current career goals. I was performing well academically, but felt lost in my Liberal Arts college where individual achievement was not acknowledged. I found several mentors who encouraged me to obtain a degree in marketing. I remained interested in health care, working as a Cardiology Technician and completing my honor's thesis in Health Care Economics. I eventually received a degree in Finance and Economics. Upon graduation, I worked as a systems analyst. I quickly realized that I could succeed financially in a business career, but I would never be happy until I became a physician.

Medical school has been exciting, challenging, and enjoyable. I found that the hard work was not a burden, but a pleasure. I earned many honors throughout my first three years, and was elected to Alpha Omega Alpha during my junior year. I also participated in many extracurricular activities including working as a Cardiology Technician, completing my M.S. in Exercise Physiology, and joining the Internal Medicine Club.

I worked as a student aide on the wards of a small hospital. The first night I fell into the rhythm of the department and was able to help patients both physically and psychologically. I felt at home in the hospital, a feeling I had never experienced before.

The clinical years have been the most rewarding. Each case has offered a new learning experience. I enjoyed every rotation, but the magnet of the Internal Medicine keeps pulling me toward it. It is as diverse as it is exciting. The wide variety of problems requires a constant vigilance and provides an opportunity to learn greater than that of any other specialty. It requires leadership and technical skills as well as a broad knowledge base. Internists are the physician's physician.

As I walk through the sand to the top of the hill I must select one of many paths to my home. Some are direct, while others have many twists and turns. I choose the trail that I will most enjoy and on which I can be the most useful. I know that the path I have chosen is the right one for me.

As the sun sets, I know I am walking home, literally to my future as an Internist and as a person.

Stanley Y. Lu

Cardiac arrests, major trauma, childbirths, dramatic operations–these are the elements most people think of when they envision medicine. Not me. The most dramatic event during my medical school years was when, after taking a history and doing a physical examination on a middle-aged woman presenting with complaints of lethargy and occasional dizziness, I was able to explain that these symptoms were caused by a medication she was taking. With the help of my attending, we switched her to a different medication. Two weeks later she returned "to me" for follow-up. She was much better, was able to resume her work and household duties, and she took my hand as she thanked me. My knowledge of pharmacology (and ability to use the PDR) allowed me to radically alter this woman's life. That is how I want to practice medicine–Internal Medicine.

I almost didn't get into medical school. Although I was born in the United States, English wasn't my first language. I didn't learn English until I entered school, and something about the combination of Chinese and English didn't fit too well. I became an unrecognized dyslexic. Yet I did well by memorizing everything I needed, often from lectures, during high school. Only when my grades plummeted in college was the disorder diagnosed and treated. This experience led me to greatly respect both the astute clinician and the healer. In my case, they did so well that I was able to take the MCAT (and do well) without any special reading assistance. After that, medical school was (relatively) easy.

My friends characterize me as a "bookworm." Perhaps that is because I am always carrying around a book to read (often non-medical). Actually, I find that medical school has a lot of "down time." Not liking to waste time or to be frustrated by waiting, I simply open the book and continue reading. It's amazing how much knowledge one can get this way.

As seems clear from my orientation, I am primarily seeking an Internal Medicine program with a solid primary care base. While I want to round this out with adequate subspecialty experiences, I need a thorough grounding in outpatient medicine. Three particular aspects are important to me: a continuity clinic where I can see the same patients over a period of time, clinical teaching from the faculty, and esprit-de-corps among the housestaff. With this training, I plan to be not a good, but a great Internist.

Lawrence J. Stanley

For as long as I can remember, I wanted to be a lawyer. Then why am I in medical school applying for an Internal Medicine residency, you may ask. I can only answer that I saw the error of my ways. I decided my life should be spent helping, rather than hindering, others.

When I entered undergraduate school, my goal was still to study law. As part of a required physical education course, I learned CPR. Little did I realize that less than a week later I would use it to save a child who nearly drowned at a neighbor's swimming pool. That got me to thinking. What did I really want out of a career? The answer was to help others in need by practicing medicine. My enjoyment of medical school, especially the clinical years, has proven that to be true.

Not that I was a star in medical school. Having basically a non-science orientation throughout high school and my early years of college, I found it somewhat difficult to catch up in my pre-clinical years. My grades reflect that. Yet in my clinical rotations I began to shine, and received excellent comments from all of my preceptors.

Why Internal Medicine? I love the idea of caring for people over the long haul. The diagnoses and treatments encompassed by Internal Medicine fascinate me, especially some of the so-called "routine" problems, such as hypertension and diabetes. Enough advances seem to be occurring in these areas to make them exciting.

What am I looking for in a program? Since I am single, geography is really not a barrier. My ideal program will have a strong clinical base, both in the primary care and specialty aspects of Internal Medicine. The faculty should be readily available for on-site instruction, and there should be good esprit-de-corps among the housestaff. Since my goal is to get out there and practice good medicine, the bottom line is to get training that will prepare me to do this. Going to clinic will be so much better than going to court.

Andrew R. Jackson

While my fascination with Neurology has evolved over the past two years, my interest in medicine dates back to elementary school in rural Texas. While pursuing a bachelor's degree in chemistry and later pharmacy, I worked as a laboratory technician, an operating room technician, and a hospital pharmacy intern to pay expenses. Each subsequent experience took me further into the patient care arena and led me to realize that I enjoyed patient contact. It seemed that all my previous science study coalesced into medicinal chemistry and clinical pharmacology. Pharmacy seemed to be an intellectually satisfying occupation in which I could work.

After graduating from pharmacy school in 1986, I completed a hospital pharmacy residency at Tuba City P.H.S. Indian Medical Center on the Navajo Indian Reservation. I assumed the newly created position of Assistant Chief Pharmacist for Field Health and Clinical Pharmacy Services. I worked on projects such as the development of chemotherapy preparation protocols, an aminoglycoside kinetics and dosing program, and improved the pharmacy's involvement in the emergency room and on internal medicine work rounds. I also established an outpatient pharmacy to support a remote family practice clinic on the Navajo Reservation. It was during this period of working closely with physicians that I recognized my desire for more meaningful interactions with patients, and for more direct involvement in diagnostic and therapeutic decisions.

This familiarity and enjoyment of patient contact made the clinical years of medical school very much like "going back to work." The clinical years have allowed me to hone skills I already possessed. In addition, when given the opportunity to apply information gleaned from my basic science courses to actual clinical situations, I found the intellectual stimulation which I desired.

My interest in Neurology began during my third-year neurology clerkship. I was impressed with the elegance of the neurological examination, and the precision with which a lesion could be methodically localized. The detective-like strategy employed to obtain a neurological diagnosis particularly appeals to me.

My professional goals center around a Clinical Neurology group practice, preferably with a strong academic affiliation, since I am also interested in teaching. My primary consideration at this point is residency training that will provide a strong background in clinical neurology as the basis for both future study and clinical practice. I seek a residency program that will impart a dynamic balance of clinical expertise, facility for inquiry, and compassion for the patient.

Philippe Ariés

✦✦

Aesop's fable of the tortoise and the hare comes to mind to describe my route into medicine. When I immigrated to the United States from a small city in France at the age of seventeen, I immediately entered public school. What a shock! My "passable English" really wasn't very good and for the first time in my life I wasn't at the top of my class. With diligent work, I improved my English to the point where I got into college to study biochemistry, as a preparation for medical school. Once again, however, I found that my English ability was not initially up to the challenge. (One professor asked why I didn't "make it easy on myself" and major in French literature!) However, I persevered. By my sophomore year, I began to reach my potential; in the third year I did great. My overall grade-point average, though, continued to reflect the difficulties I had the first year, and I failed to get accepted at any U.S. medical school. I was furious. I was bewildered. Most of all, I was depressed. I decided to take some time off.

During the next six years I had many interesting experiences. Among other things, I helped explore for oil off the Kuril Islands, led treks through Sri Lanka (before the civil war), worked in a French-owned laboratory in Tunis, and qualified as a professional diver. These jobs were interesting, were often dangerous, and took me to places most people had never heard of, let alone visited. Yet I was unsatisfied. I was supposed to be a physician; I needed to be a physician. So, I tried again.

Again, I had no luck with U.S. schools, but I got accepted to St. George's University School of Medicine in Grenada. I started there, but something funny happened in my second year—we got invaded by the United States (and they may have saved our lives). I, and many of my colleagues, took a forced hiatus. I eventually returned to Grenada and finished medical school, taking all of my clinical rotations at U.S. hospitals. I also passed the exams needed for my ECFMG certification and completed a transitional internship at the Washington Adventist Hospital, Takoma Park, Maryland in 1988. Since then, I have practiced at a small industrial medicine clinic in the Washington, D.C. area. Now, however, I want to complete a formal residency training program.

Preventive Medicine and Rehabilitation seems the natural choice for me. Much of what I have been doing in the past several years falls within this scope of practice. I find that I have a gift for diagnosing and treating neuromuscular diseases, as well as helping people make adjustments to continue their work. What I need now is to get more education in the area than I have been able to glean from reading books and articles. For that reason, this tortoise is finally applying to PM & R residencies. If accepted, I, too, will make Aesop proud.

✦✦

Assad L. Sayah, M.D.

The practice of medicine encompasses what is best in man and brings out the best in those who practice its art. I have found that to be true for me. Now that I am in the United States, I hope that I can continue my practice of medicine.

I was born in Lebanon and attended the American University of Beirut. After graduating from medical school, I did a 12-month rotating internship at the general hospital. While I formally rotated through Pediatrics, Surgery, Medicine, and Preventive Medicine/Public Health, much of my time was, because of the war, spent in the Emergency Department. It was a time for rapid learning and quickly taking enormous responsibility for others' lives. When I completed this year, thanks to relatives in the United States, I was able to immigrate.

After arriving in the United States, I completed clerkships at the University of North Carolina at Chapel Hill, in Radiation Oncology, Medical Oncology, and Otolaryngologic Oncology. Each lasted four months. I chose these clerkships from those available because of my interest in Oncology. I wanted to see how it was really practiced in the United States and which aspect of it I was most interested in. During this period I passed all of the tests for my ECFMG on my first try. This was not difficult, since my English is very good (my parents had made us speak it at home ever since we were small), and we had studied from American textbooks at school.

I am now ready to embark on my formal residency training in Oncology—specifically Radiation Oncology. This field offers me an opportunity to combine my knowledge and interest in physics and mathematics with compassionate patient care. In addition, this field seems to be one that is developing at an exponential rate and it should provide me with the intellectual stimulation I require. Eventually, I would like to enter academic medicine and teach Radiation Oncology to others, as well as periodically returning to Lebanon to instruct our physicians in the most advanced techniques.

Although my background appears somewhat strange, I can assure you that, if selected for your program, I will be a graduate of whom you can be proud.

MARK ANTHONY

Who is Mark Anthony, and what do you want to know about him? My typical day is frenetic, chaotic, and very rewarding. It combines medical school with family life, trying to become a doctor, and trying to be a good father and husband. This evening, my wife of six years is thirty-eight weeks pregnant with our second child. The backaches and contractions have begun and we suspect she will deliver within a few days. Polly, our four-year-old, continuously asks the unanswerable question, such as "Does God have a mother?" while getting into every drawer, closet, and cabinet that hasn't been child-proofed. Not content with just having children, my wife sits here proofreading her Ph.D. thesis in applied physics (while trying to answer Polly's questions). I try to reread Harrison's section on thyroid diseases. Both of us are partially successful.

On most days, I go to the hospital early to do rounds before the residents. Arriving early, staying late, and doing anything that's needed for patient care has stood me in good stead on all of my rotations. It has also given me opportunities I otherwise may have missed, such as running a resuscitation until the "code team" arrived, first-assisting the Chief of Surgery on an emergency appendectomy, and doing procedures on our team's patients after everyone but the resident and I had left for the day.

What I want most from my medical career is to use all of my knowledge in the best possible way. Since I seem to excel at both diagnostic and procedural skills, I want my career to encompass both. This led me, naturally, to Radiology (probably Interventional). I have spent time with radiologists to learn more about the specialty, staying with them to take after-hours call, during an elective month, and attending both the state and national radiology meetings. I'm sold!

I should mention my stable, 80% bilateral hearing loss, due to a childhood illness. I compensate by using hearing aids and lip-reading. I always attended public schools and am considered to have excellent speech. In clinical practice, an enhanced stethoscope allows me to hear heart, lung, bowel, and vascular sounds as well as any other clinician.

Ten years from now I see myself with a large family, an exciting position in Radiology, and a respected position in my community. With your help, I'll get there.

Julie Wang

"Officer down!" came the voice over the scanner. A fellow police officer had been shot while trying to arrest a robbery suspect. After we had arrested the suspect, a paramedic provided initial care to the wounded officer. I still remember the officer, pale, lying in a pool of blood with a tortured look on his face. He was rushed to surgery and underwent a small bowel resection. I remember wanting to be in the operating room, wanting to see what was happening and, above all, wanting to help. I was impressed by the surgeon's skills and compassion as the officer recovered. This incident, like so many others involving injured victims or suspects, stimulated me to pursue a career as a physician.

At an early age, I became fascinated by physiology, pathology, and anatomy. Although I dreamed of becoming a physician, I thought this goal was beyond my reach and considered other career options that offered the same personal interaction. I became a police officer because it allowed me to assist others, use my leadership skills, and work with diverse groups of people in intense problem-solving situations. It was an active, demanding career that I enjoyed not only for what I learned about others, but for the strengths and abilities that I found in myself. After working for a number of years as a patrol officer, I felt the need for a more intellectually challenging career, and returned to college. As I pursued a degree in biology, my interest in medicine was reinforced. I volunteered in a hospital to learn the realities of a physician's professional life. Interacting with physicians helped me realize that I possessed the intellectual maturity, sound judgment, and confidence necessary to be an excellent doctor. Thus I applied to medical school to pursue my dream of becoming a physician.

When I entered medical school, I had a strong interest in surgery. I kept an open mind about other disciplines but none interested me as much as surgery. I am most attracted by the active role surgeons have in changing a patient's condition. I enjoy assessing problems, developing strategies to solve them and using my hands to carry out these strategies. The logical and methodical problem-solving strategies of surgery are well suited to my abilities. During the third year of medical school, my favorite moments were learning procedures and performing them on my own. I thrive on the sense of accomplishment obtained after exceeding what I perceive as my capabilities. I enjoy seeing the results of my work and learning if my diagnosis was correct, which is possible in surgery, since the patient's condition often changes and improves quickly. Surgery provides a diversity of patients and diagnoses in an ever-changing clinical environment. Surgery permits me to use my interpersonal skills to establish rapport with patients and calm their fears.

During my first years in medical school, I found that the stress management and learning skills I developed as a police officer helped me to earn honors in difficult courses. I have continued to take a leadership role in medical school. Last year I was nominated by my class and appointed by the Dean to the College of Medicine's Admissions Committee. As Secretary-Treasurer of our American Medical Students Association chapter, I conducted two very successful used-book sales. I use my communication and interpersonal skills as a peer counselor for my fellow medical students. I conducted two clinical research projects in dermatology and found research to be an excellent way to learn about a subject in a practical and theoretical manner. I will participate in surgical research this fall and winter.

My career goals include clinical practice in association with an academic institution. Teaching appeals to me: I like sharing information and learning from those that I teach. With my past work experience as a police officer and my performance in medical school, I have obtained the necessary skills to be an outstanding surgeon. I am looking for a program that will allow enhance my present skills and provide me with an excellent surgical education.

Albert Jonson, M.D.

I wish to enroll in a Cardiology fellowship for three reasons. First, data clearly show that many people suffer from cardiovascular problems due to unhealthy lifestyles. Second, my training in nutrition and physical education equips me to teach patients about changes that can prevent cardiovascular problems. Third, I enjoy working with healthy and ill patients, and I want to learn how to better help both groups of people enjoy personal wellness. For me, these aspects define Cardiology.

Academically, I remain curious about cardiovascular physiology and pathology, especially patients who don't seem to "have read the textbook" and whose symptomatology and disease course doesn't follow discernible patterns. Currently, I am conducting a study to determine the effects of post-MI exercise and diet changes on cholesterol levels. I want to participate in research on the relationship between hypertension, diabetes, and heart disease. I also enjoy teaching. This past year, for example, the graduating medical students voted me the top teaching resident. I believe my concern, communication skills, and quest for sharing knowledge contributed to my receiving this award.

My Internal Medicine background has given me a strong knowledge base in nutrition and problem-solving. I want to learn more about preventive health measures and how to help people make lifestyle changes. My personal challenge with weight control has made me realize the importance of family support in improving the health of patients with cardiovascular disease. Therefore, I want to learn how to involve the entire family in a person's wellness efforts. I seek a Cardiology fellowship that will help me learn more about these issues.

Florence Nightingale, R. N.

Although three of my siblings entered medical school, I felt that my calling was in nursing. My role was to comfort and care for patients. For the past seven years I have done that, first on the medical-surgical wards, and then as a home-health nurse. As my career proceeded, I found myself not only acquiring many new skills, but desperately wanting more. Finally, the light dawned—it was time to take the next step and enter a nurse-practitioner program.

What do I plan to accomplish as a nurse-practitioner? Actually, I suspect that many of my patients will be similar to the ones I have now. My commitment to home health and hospice work remains strong, and I believe a nurse practitioner could do wonderful things in this environment which is often shunned by physicians. In fact, several hospice programs in the area have already approached me with offers to sponsor me during school if I will work with them when I graduate. That would help enormously, since I am not exactly rich.

Aside from nursing, my life centers around my extensive family. My husband, a bank vice president and computer guru, and I have been together for ten years. We have three children, ages eight, six, and four. Luckily for me, my husband and I share equally in the care of our children, which will free up time that I will need for school. We have even made arrangements to have a part-time nanny so I will have additional time for school work.

All is, of course, not work. As a family, we take frequent "educational" trips. Some of these involve camping (my husband's passion), while others are trips to museums, art galleries (my love), or even Disney World (we all enjoyed it). With our two oldest in school, we both also actively participate in school activities, including working with the PTA, volunteering as teachers' aides, and attending all of the children's plays and choral performances. We also play music as a family (adequately), with Janice, the littlest one, beginning to hit the drum a bit more in rhythm recently.

I look forward to beginning this new aspect of my nursing career. More importantly, perhaps, my future employers and some of my current patients are anxious for me to begin. It should be great for all of us.

Robert J. Openheimer, M.D.

I once tried sky diving. I thought it great fun–once I got out the door of the plane. Eventually, my instructor said, "Bob, you really don't like going through that door very much, do you?" He was right and that was my last jump. My wife, too, is a very perceptive person. Several months ago she handed me a copy of *Getting Into A Residency* when I came home from the office. "What's this for?" I asked laughingly. "You've been complaining for several years that you aren't happy doing ENT, so if you're serious, make another choice and go for it," she replied. I was flabbergasted, but also relieved that she would go through the travail of another residency with me again.

I did not need the book to help select a specialty (only to go through the mechanics of application and interviewing). I already knew what I wanted to do–Family Practice. My problem with ENT is that the field, at least for me, is too narrow. I am doing general ENT, with some facial plastics, oncology, complicated ear problems, and lots of dizziness. Yet my goal is really to be the complete physician, taking care of people over the long haul. As with many medical students, my interest in Otolaryngology was piqued by a great clinician with whom I came in contact. He had a wonderful bedside manner, interesting and grateful patients, and an enthusiastic group of intelligent and able residents. Mistakenly, I didn't think any further than that, and applied only to ENT programs.

Now I find that I miss the continuity of care, the broad range of medical, surgical, obstetric, and psychiatric problems I was exposed to as a student. My days have become very routine, which troubles me greatly, since I have only been out of residency four years. My real calling is Family Practice, and I (and my wife) are willing to sacrifice to make this dream come about.

Not only will I bring enthusiasm to any Family Practice program, but I can also bring my in-depth knowledge of ENT, a major part of any Family Physician's practice. My surgical skills should help me greatly, as will my experience with pediatric patients. I will, of course, clearly be playing catch-up with those just out of medical school in the areas of Psychiatry, Obstetrics and Gynecology, and Medicine. I look forward to the challenge.

What I ultimately seek is to return to my community as a caring, well-trained Family Physician. I'll finally be where I belong.

GERTRUDE STEIN, M.D.

Medicine is more than a career; it is a calling. Few professionals must assume as much responsibility for human life or derive as much personal satisfaction from their work. All the major decisions in my life have been made with one goal in mind: to be the best physician I could be. As time goes on, my objective has become clearer and more defined.

Nothing is static. Dreams and goals may change, but I can say with assurance that I would like to spend my life being challenged by different situations. Encountering new people and new problems is always invigorating. After much consideration, I have decided to enter Obstetrics and Gynecology.

A diverse background is an asset in any specialty. My engineering background at Cal Tech helps me think deductively, and has proved repeatedly useful when evaluating symptomatology that does not fit textbook cases. My additional training and graduate teaching in Comparative Literature helped me hone my communication skills and become comfortable working with people from diverse social and cultural backgrounds.

Research experience taught me to read papers, understand methodology, examine the results, and draw my own conclusions–as well as to raise new questions the authors had not examined. This provides the basis for my own clinical practice and eventually, my research.

The past two years in a General Surgery residency should be a useful asset in Ob/Gyn. My skills in assessing surgical patients, treating perioperative problems, and doing surgical procedures has constantly been considered excellent. Yet I find myself unfulfilled.

What continues to excite me is Obstetrics and Gynecology. In medical school, I waffled between it and Surgery. Almost immediately I knew I had erred in not selecting Ob/Gyn. Even as a surgical resident, my most rewarding experience was a two-month elective in Gynecological Surgery. In the little spare time I had, I began volunteering to help deliver babies. (My OB colleagues were ever so grateful.) This simply reassured me that I needed to enter Ob/Gyn. And now, despite the increased length of my training, that is what I plan to do. Obstetrics and Gynecology is my calling.

11: Cover and Thank-You Letters

Cover and thank-you letters are like icing on a cake.

The job is not over until the paperwork is done

A polished résumé and personal statement are important, but you need to "put some icing on the cake." Before your interview, the *cover letter*, attached to the front of your application packet, is usually the first thing reviewers see. After an interview the committee meets to discuss applicants (remember, the committee will review applicants other than you), and make their selections. A thank-you letter sent to interviewers immediately after your visit keeps your memory fresh in their minds. It's a sound strategy to make yourself stand out in both situations. This chapter will help you write impressive cover and thank-you letters.

What is a cover letter?

A cover letter concisely expresses your interest in a position and states why you want that position. It is usually attached to the front of your application packet. Let's examine the definition more closely

- *Concisely expresses your interest in a position.* Your cover letter should emphatically state the specific title (even include the advertisement number, if available) of the position for which you are applying. Put that information in the *first paragraph* to ensure that anyone in the company or institution can identify the job you want. Say something like:

    I am applying for the Dental Assistant position in your company that was recently advertised in the *Sun Times.*

- *States why you want that position.* Honestly explain any factors that motivated you to apply for the position. The desire to live closer to family members, the need for more responsibility, and the opportunity to better use your skills are some reasons people desire new and, hopefully, better positions. Avoid being too direct. Instead, emphasize that you want, for example, a "challenging position that will allow me to use my health care expertise in a supervisory capacity."

- *Don't say* "I want the position because I need more money." (You may know the position's salary range, but don't mention salary until after you've been offered the position.)

    > Oliver, a medical technologist, had lived in Charlotte, North Carolina for eight years. Although he and his family liked the Charlotte area, Oliver and Joan, his spouse, had discussed relocating to San Antonio so they could be close to Joan's aging parents. Oliver and Joan finally decided to make the move. Oliver asked his relatives to look for Med Tech positions in the local newspaper and in local jobs listings. Through them he learned of several interesting positions in the San Antonio area. He decided to apply for them. His résumé reflected his expertise, but since no personal statement was requested, Oliver wondered how to tell the reviewers why he wanted to move. He finally wrote a cover letter (Figure 11.1) that expressed his rationale. He had several interviews and was hired for one of the positions.

Look at Oliver's cover letter in figure 11.1. Notice that Oliver concisely stated that he wanted the job and discussed why. He directly commented on the "match" between the position's supervisory duties and his skills. Also, he smoothly suggested an interview by listing the dates he would be in San Antonio and providing "in-town" contact information (material not included on Oliver's résumé). Oliver *did not*

- leave any doubt as to the position he wanted.

- beg for the position.

Figure 11.1. Oliver's Cover Letter

Oliver O. Howard
6505 Central Avenue
Charlotte, North Carolina 28045
(704) 555-5888

September 20, 1994

Ms. Elizabeth Seton
Senior Vice President for Personnel
Advanced Medical Enterprises
1411 Madison St.
San Antonio, TX 78214

Dear Ms. Seton:

I am applying for the Senior Medical Technologist position (Job #343) at Advanced Medical Enterprises that was advertised in the September 15th edition of the *San Antonio Express*.

The Senior Medical Technologist position interests me for two reasons. First, the position's duties involve supervision, an area in which I have acquired skills through on-the-job training and college courses. Second, my family and I want to relocate to San Antonio so that we can be closer to my spouse's elderly parents.

I will be in San Antonio from October 1 through October 30. During that time I can be contacted at the home of John and Mary Thompson, 555-6768. I would like to discuss the position with you at your convenience. My résumé is attached.

Sincerely yours,

Oliver O. Howard, M.T., (ASCP)

Attachment: Résumé

- re-write his résumé in the cover letter. (I've seen some cover letters that were longer than the applicant's résumé.)

- write a 2 to 3 page cover letter describing his supervisory skills in great detail.

In summary, while you shouldn't spend hours on a cover letter, do write a polished letter that clearly and concisely relays pertinent information. Also include the reasons you desire the position.

What is a thank-you letter?

A "thank-you" letter is a short, written note that expresses your appreciation for the consideration given to you during the interview Specifically, it says "thanks" for the interview (meals, lodging, etc.), expresses your continued interest in the position, mentions specific interviewers, and asks if the selection committee needs additional information. In short, a "thank-you letter" is the icing on the cake (interview).

Thank-you letters are important. They can mean the difference between selection and the other alternative.

> Margaret, a fourth-year medical student, was interviewed at a family medicine residency program in rural Iowa. Margaret really liked the program's residents, attendings, educational opportunities, and physical facilities. She especially liked the rural setting and the opportunity to establish ties in the small community. During the interview, residents and attendings emphasized that the program was far from a large city and its attractions. In fact, the program director told all applicants that some residents had left the program because they felt isolated in such a rural setting. Margaret listed this program first among her choices for the residency Match, but she never expressed her interest, in writing, to anyone in the program. Later, when Margaret failed to "match" and had to "scramble" for a position, she telephoned that program's director to determine why they had not selected her. To her surprise, the program director said that everyone liked her, but they thought that she was not interested in the program so they failed to rank her among their list of choices. Fortunately for Margaret, one position was unfilled at that program, and she immediately accepted the position when it was offered.

In Margaret's case, a simple "thank-you" letter (see Figure 11.2) might have saved her a great deal of anxiety. Surely, the program could have contacted her and asked if she were really interested. But is this really the program's responsibility? The issue of how much to encourage applicants, challenges training programs and companies. One attending told me that the faculty in his program debated for hours about what to tell applicants. An interview follow-up letter from the program that was "too strong" might raise false expectations among some applicants. On the other hand, either no letter or a "plain vanilla" letter might discourage all applicants–even the people the program *really* wanted. Don't risk a misunderstanding, invest your time preparing a well-written, personal letter that "ices" the cake.

Figure 11.2. Thank-You Letter That Margaret Should Have Written

Margaret C. Nga
5560 East Parkway
Houston, Texas 77226
(713) 555-2310

November 15, 1994

Martha C. Olson, M.D.
Family Medicine Residency Program Director
Derby Community Hospital
Derby, Iowa 50375

Dear Dr. Olson:

Thank you for the courtesies extended to me during my interview last Friday. Your program's atmosphere was warm and inviting, and I appreciate the way everyone made me feel at ease. I especially enjoyed the lunch with the residents.

I left the interview with a very positive feeling. Our discussion of health care needs in rural settings reminded me of a preceptorship I completed in rural Texas following my second year in medical school. I thoroughly enjoyed that experience, and welcome the opportunity to get to know patients as people the way I did in that environment. Please tell Dr. Mike McGill how much I liked our discussion about AIDS education in local high schools. I enjoyed hearing of the challenges the program faced when it began. Also, please thank Mr. James Madison, your administrative assistant, for arranging for my transportation to and from the airport.

Again, I had a very pleasant interview at your program. The setting and the learning climate attract me, and your program fulfills what I seek in my residency training. Please contact me if I can supply you with additional information.

Sincerely yours,

Margaret C. Nga
MS IV

The sample letter in Figure 11.2 concisely thanks the program for the interview, mentions key people with whom Margaret met, details their mutual interests, and confirms her interest in the position. Notice that the letter *does not*

- beg for a position.

- get too glowing about either Margaret or the program.

- discuss at length that Margaret liked every aspect of the program.

- sound like a "generic" form letter that Margaret sent to all programs.

- fake enthusiasm for the program.

Margaret should have mailed the thank-you letter immediately following the interview. Doing this reduces memory slips and the chances of confusing programs or interviewers. She could easily have written the letter on her flight home or on the way to her next interview. She could have even mailed the letter at the airport.

One applicant related to me that she wrote her thank-you letters in her hotel (often using the hotel's office typewriter) as soon as she finished her interviews for the day. The hotel staff didn't always appreciate this, but her interviewers were impressed with how quickly they received these notes.

Margaret could have also sent Mike McGill and James Madison separate thank-you letters. Those letters should focus on the interviewer, rather than on the program.

What if you don't want to say "thank you"?

Should you send a thank-you letter if you think you were unfairly treated in an interview? My experience (and what I've heard from hundreds of health professions students and job applicants) is that health care professionals realize that interviews are stressful for everyone and want to make the experience as pleasant as possible. After all, they want to attract good people to their programs or institutions. Yet, there is usually the "one in every crowd." You know who I'm describing–the person who torments you with all those detailed questions and seems to enjoy making life uncomfortable for other people. Expect this person and deal with him or her as pleasantly as possible. You might also have been disappointed by broader issues, such as a lack of coordination or planning during an interview.

What should you do if, after the interview visit, you decide you really don't want that position? Its up to you, but I recommend that, in this case, you do not send a thank-you letter. You may send a "generic" letter, if you wish, just to be polite. *Do not,* however, tell a program or a company about its weaknesses or say you are still interested in the position.

Summary about thank-you letters

In summary, a well-written and timely thank-you letter may influence whether you are selected for a position. The time and effort it takes to write a thank-you letter are small investments considering the potential return. After working so hard on your application materials, traveling to a site, and interviewing, the ten minutes you spend writing a thank-you letter puts the "icing" on your efforts.

12: Building/Strengthening Your Résumé and Personal Statement

Plan experiences to build your résumé and personal statement.

Building/strengthening your résumé and personal statement

Review your résumé and personal statement. If you followed the steps suggested in this book, your materials should accurately reflect who you are, your experiences, and your marketable attributes. Hopefully, you are pleased with your résumé and personal statement. Even if you are satisfied with your accomplishments up to now, however, you must work to acquire additional marketable strengths to continue growing as a person and for career advancement.

Eleanor completed her family medicine residency in Texas and accepted a faculty position in Utah. After moving, making new friends, and adjusting to the demands of her new job, Eleanor was ready for new challenges. Her goal was to advance further in the academic world. Eleanor's department chair encouraged her to participate in a Family Medicine Faculty Development Program in which she polished her teaching skills, completed a research project, presented her results at the annual Society for Teachers of Family Medicine Conference, and met other professionals who shared her interests in teaching. She also worked with a mentor who gave her helpful career advice. Eleanor's résumé grew so as to advance her career.

You, like Eleanor, can grow as a health care professional and a person. *This chapter will help you formulate a plan to build or strengthen your résumé and personal statement.* It describes a strategy to acquire experiences, skills, and abilities through planned activities. It suggests ways to set goals, describes tactics to attain those goals, and illustrates ways to record your successes. It also cites examples of how others built or strengthened their résumés and personal statements.

One sure thing about the future is that it is uncertain. People change, and so do their career goals and choices. A sound way to deal with this uncertainly is to increase your options. Opportunities don't appear magically, they are created. Read this chapter to get ideas that can help you develop the necessary skills for your career. If you are a:

- *Future physician.* Seek activities to develop the knowledge, skills, and attributes sought by medical or osteopathic schools. For example, Janet, in her second year of undergraduate school, served as an officer in several campus groups. She developed leadership, delegation, and organizational skills while maintaining excellent grades. She later entered osteopathic school.

- *First-year medical or osteopathic student.* Begin to develop attributes to market yourself to residency programs. Curtis became fascinated with the head and neck while studying gross anatomy as a first-year medical student. He attended ENT conferences, networked with otolaryngologists, scrubbed for head and neck surgeries, and co-authored an article in an ENT journal with his mentor. He documented this long-term interest in the specialty on his résumé and personal statement. He was accepted into the ENT residency program of his choice.

- *Pre-pharmacy or other pre-health sciences program student.* Develop your skills and acquire experience with professionals in your future vocation. George worked as a pharmacy technician for three years. He used computers, interacted with professional staff, and developed an in-depth knowledge about prescription medications. When he completed his pre-pharmacy coursework and applied to pharmacy school, his application materials reflected his expertise, experience, and desire to practice pharmacy. He was accepted into pharmacy school and went on to complete his Doctor of Pharmacy degree.

- *Future applicant to another professional school.* Identify and obtain the skills that will make you a marketable candidate. Many health care professionals later enter other professional programs such as law school. They frequently cite their health care experiences in their personal statements. Scott trained as a radiological technologist in the military. Although he liked his job, he wanted more responsibility, a larger income, and a career in which he could use his science background. Scott enrolled in classes to develop his reading and writing skills, talked with attorneys to learn what they actually did, and became an officer in a school pre-law club. He later entered law school and now works as an attorney for a major medical center.

- *Allied health professions student.* Identify professional opportunities that are available to you. Develop contacts with professional in your field by joining professional organizations and attending meetings. Volunteer to work in your area of interest. Glenda, a med technology student, worked part-time in a chemistry laboratory to put herself through school. She quickly developed her bench skills and formed a network of mentors at the university's hospital. Upon graduation, she was offered a full-time job in the chemistry lab.

- *Medical or osteopathic resident.* Explore future career options and develop the skills necessary for those you might pursue. Do you want to practice in an academic health sciences center or a community hospital? Learn what is expected in each setting and identify each option's pros and cons. If you fail to plan, things might not work out too well. Stuart completed medical school and his pediatrics residency at the same institution. He was highly recruited by several pediatrics departments in university-based programs. Stuart accepted a position in a program about 1,500 miles from his medical school. Unfortunately, he failed to obtain much information about the job requirements in advance. He also failed to find a suitable mentor in his new location. He was overwhelmed by his clinical load and became frustrated when he couldn't find the time and energy to write grants and conduct clinical research. After three years, Stuart left the position feeling defeated and frustrated.

- *At any career level.* Develop any skills you think will help you in the future. As you've seen earlier in this book, any experience can develop or hone your marketable attributes. You may think that you never want to change jobs, switch specialty areas, or go to school again, but circumstances have a way of changing. You might feel differently in the future. Mary Lou was a med tech for eleven years. During this time she swore that she never wanted to go to school again. Yet, after a move across the country, she could find no job which appealed to her. She decided to go to law school and work in the medico-legal field. Skills she had developed in research, such as discipline and time-management, helped her win acceptance to law school, and to complete it near the top of her class.

- *Graduate school (e.g., MPH program)*. The academic knowledge you're gaining is great. Future employers, especially for that all-important first job, will look to see what practical experience you have. Do you have any? Nancy, an MPH student knew that she would want to get into the public health field as quickly as possible after completing her degree. She arranged to volunteer, and then to get a part-time job at her county's health clinic. When she applied for her first job after completing her degree, potential employers were impressed that she already had practical experience.

- *Employment at non-academic organizations*. Do you want to progress in your job responsibility, position and salary? Of course you do. What special skills will get you there? What skills can you develop that will be needed by your current or a similar employer in the future? Bruce saw that the future of health care was inextricably linked to computers. He took some courses at night to develop his computer skills and had the added pleasure of "surfing" the Internet. His employer quickly recognized his computer abilities and promoted him to a position where he could use them most effectively.

Muscle, not padding

When I mention building or strengthening résumés or personal statements, some people misinterpret what I mean. They think I'm suggesting that they inflate, exaggerate, or misrepresent their accomplishments (i.e., "pad" their documents) so that they will increase their likelihood of obtaining interviews. "Padding" is a self-defeating technique. Even if a "padder" initially outfoxes an admissions or personnel committee and gets an interview, some astute interviewer will probably ask questions that uncover the exaggerated attributes or skills. Honesty is the best policy.

DEVELOPING A LONG-TERM STRATEGY

Developing yourself and strengthening your résumé and personal statement go together. *A well-planned self-development strategy should simultaneously help you and others. It should be a "win-win" situation for all involved.* As you peer into the future, identify the specific marketable attributes you will need. Then engage in activities that will help you acquire them. This strategy should help you advance along your career path.

Tom, now a pre-med student, is applying to the military to be a corpsman. He is currently an EMT, and is taking paramedic training to further his skills. This should help him in the military. Since his career goal is to be a physician, the military training and experience as a medical corpsman will enhance his chances of being accepted into medical school.

In the last part of Chapter 6 you identified the attributes sought by selection or admissions committees. Then in Chapters 7 and 8, you assessed your attributes and identified the matches and the mismatches between your skills and those reviewers seek. The outcome was your marketing strategy listing the strengths you could emphasize to programs or employers.

Applying now

If you are submitting an application now, use the rest of this book to put together your résumé and personal statement. By doing this, you will identify the skills you currently have. You will probably get some ideas of skills to develop or hone as well.

You will likely list attributes like leadership, organizational skills, and team-building skills. George (described above) applied for pharmacy school. He had excelled in science courses and had developed leadership, communication, and computer skills during his first two years of college. His academic accomplishments were highly desired, but his other traits made him an even more competitive candidate. His concrete experiences proved that he could lead and work with others. His volunteer experiences with service and community groups helped develop his marketable traits while he helped others.

Applying in the future

If you plan to submit an application in the future, you still have time to develop skills and strengthen your application packet. (Even if you are not planning on changing jobs, career advancement requires new skills too.) Faced with intense competition, applicants who demonstrate marketable skills have a distinct advantage when compared with applicants who lack those attributes. The positive impact of planned experiences may be the deciding factor to a reviewer reading stacks of applications. Use the steps below to form your own plan for developing skills.

❑ 1. *Identify traits sought in applicants.* Review the last part of Chapter 6. Get valid and reliable information about the characteristics sought by those who will review your application. Use a *variety of sources* for this information. Don't rely strictly on one source. Review catalogs and promotional literature, talk with admissions directors or prospective employers, speak with your advisor or mentor, form a network with others who are currently in the program or position in which you want to enroll. Scan journals in relevant areas, and attend professional meetings (professionals will usually invite you to attend). Grades as well as scores on standardized tests (like the MCAT) are important. Special skills, like signing or speaking a second language, may also set you apart. Volunteer work, teaching or research experiences, or administrative duties are also great skill builders. Specialized experiences, like working in a laboratory or on an ambulance, can also make you look more attractive to selection committees.

❑ 2. *Assess yourself.* Use Chapters 3, 7, and 8 to assess and prioritize your experiences and marketable attributes. What attributes would you market to an

Figure 12.1: Chris' Initial Table of Skills

Unique ("Stand-out") Skills	Skills to Develop
1. Leadership skills	1. Time management skills
2. Team-building skills	2. Organizational skills
3. Communication skills	3. Group presentation skills

employer if you applied today? Everyone has some skills that they could strengthen. What attributes do you lack? How can you develop them? Begin now to acquire them. Look at the table (figure 12.1) that Chris, a second-year osteopathic student prepared. He labeled the columns: *"Unique ("stand-out") Skills"* and *"Skills to Develop."* He then completed the table.

❑ 3. *Check for accuracy and completeness.* Ask a trusted friend or mentor to critique your table. Sometimes others can see skills we have that we overlook. In other instances they might question the skills we think we possess or suggest additional areas to develop.

Chris discussed his list in figure 12.1 with his advisor, who suggested that Chris often spent too much time in his leadership positions because he did everything himself. Chris agreed and added "delegation skills" to the skills to develop. (Actually, after developing his delegation skills Chris' concerns about his time management and organizational skills were reduced.) In addition, his advisor suggested that Chris add Spanish-speaking skills to his "Skills to Develop" list because Chris wanted to move to the southwestern United States. Chris revised his list as shown in figure 12.2.

Figure 12.2: Chris' Revised Table of Skills

Unique ("Stand-out") Skills	Skills to Develop
1. Leadership skills	1. *Delegation skills*
2. Team-building skills	2. *Spanish-speaking skills*
3. Communication skills	3. *Group presentation skills*

❑ 4. *Complete your own table.* A number of skills you might want to develop are listed below. Put those you need or would like to acquire or polish in the appropriate columns of your table below. (Note that this is not a complete list, it is only to get you started.)

___ Fine motor skills (working with your hands)	___ Computer skills
___ Organizational skills	___ Leadership skills
___ Ability to work in a high-stress environment	___ Writing Skills
___ Delegation skills	___ Meeting skills
___ Negotiation skills	___ Research skills
___ Time management skills	___ Reading skills
___ Improved learning skills	___ Teaching skills
	___ Teaming skills
	___ Communication skills

YOUR TABLE OF SKILLS

Unique ("Stand-out") Skills	Skills to Develop

187

❏ 5. *Set goals and establish priorities.* A list does you no good unless you use it. Specific, challenging, and realistic goals keep you focused on relevant attributes. Establishing priorities helps you develop activities in a systematic and time-efficient way. Don't try to work on all your "Skills to Develop" at once. Ensure that your goals and priorities match with your future program or career needs. Chris chose "delegation skills" as his top priority, because he thought that improved delegation skills would give him extra time to spend on his studies and with his family. He put "Spanish-speaking skills" as his second priority because he knew he could take a Spanish course during the next semester.

❏ 6. *Identify activities to develop the desired attributes.* Now that you've listed the skills you want to develop, think of activities that can help you develop them. Talk to your friends, advisor, faculty, and supervisor to identify activities that are readily available.

The opportunities are there. You must find the ones that best meet your needs. I refer *pre-med students* to programs such as Med-Start, a minority student recruitment program that exposes students interested in medicine to the field through a variety of meaningful experiences. I refer *medical students* to special programs at their own schools. The Medical Student Research Program at the University of Arizona, for example, pairs students who want research experience with clinical and basic science researchers. One medical student group at Arizona, Commitment to Underserved People (CUP), staffs a refugee clinic with attendings, residents, and medical students. Your Dean of Students should be able to tell you about similar opportunities at your school. I also refer advisees to faculty who enjoy helping students or trainees develop certain skills or acquire specific experiences. Health science students and professionals in all areas have programs they can participate in which will improve their job skills.

❏ 7. *Form networks with professionals in your chosen field.* Attend local, state, and national meetings. Read in advance to learn about key issues and to identify key people in your field. Introduce yourself to others and participate in the sessions. If you currently have a mentor, keep in close contact with him or her. If you don't, find one. Mentors give career advice, link you with professional contacts, and write recommendation letters for you. These professional contacts can last for years.

❏ 8. *Form networks with classmates or peers.* Don't overlook those who are in your class at school or with whom you work. The relationships you form with these individuals often last a lifetime. *Volunteer for committees and worthwhile community-service activities.* These activities can enhance your skills, give you contact with people within and outside your career field, and use your services to assist others.

Follow your plan

❏ 9. *Do it.* Once you know what you want to do, do it! But don't *overdo* it. Follow through, contact key people, let them know what you want to do (make sure their goals and yours match), and do it. Use the telephone, personal visits, and e-mail to make and maintain contacts. Smart people know what they want. They make their opportunities happen by actively seeking them out. Then they take advantage of these opportunities to help themselves and others.

❏ 10. *Assess your progress.* Periodically, about every two months, assess your progress to determine if you are learning the skills you thought you would. (You may also be learning some skills you didn't anticipate.) If you gain something worthwhile from an activity, continue it. If you are dissatisfied for any reason, discuss it with your supervisor, mentor or other appropriate person. If the problem can be fixed, continue. But if not, you may have to gracefully quit.

> Darlene became involved in numerous extracurricular activities during her first semester in nursing school. These activities consumed a great deal of time, but she passed her courses and thought the activities balanced her academic and personal life. However, during the second semester, she found some courses more demanding than she had anticipated. Darlene thought about quitting all her extracurricular activities so she could concentrate on academics. I suggested that she balance her workload to develop some marketable attributes. She decided to quit one very time-consuming activity and reduce her commitments to two other groups. Darlene talked with each organization's advisor and explained why she needed the extra time. Each advisor understood and encouraged her to participate whenever she could.

Don't just withdraw. Informing key people of the need to cut back helps avoid hurt feelings. People understand (most have had to learn to cut back, too).

Record your accomplishments!

You will need a résumé and, in many cases, a personal statement throughout your career whenever you apply for a position in any undergraduate, professional (e.g., medicine, nursing, pharmacy, physician assistant) or graduate school, or training program, or fellowship. They are also required for scholarship and job applications. *Prepare now for your future needs. Keep these documents up-to-date.*

Make it easy. Use a systematic method to record relevant information. Otherwise, you can forget key experiences when you write or revise your résumé or personal statement. Here are a few suggestions that others have used.

- *Maintain a "Résumé and Personal Statement" file.* Dr. Frank Hale, a Family and Community Medicine colleague, suggests labeling a folder "Résumé and Personal Statement Information." Store newsletters, memos, thank-you notes, letters, and notes in the folder to record your personal accomplishments or development activities (e.g., when you were elected president of the Family

Practice Club, represented your school at an American Nursing Association conference, or had a paper published in a specialty journal). Review this folder often to see what you have done.

- *Update your résumé every six months.* A scheduled update (each January and July) should take less than thirty minutes. Rich, a first-year medical student, was a bit stressed when I met with him. He needed a résumé for a scholarship application, and the packet had to be postmarked that day. While in his case we were able to prepare a one-page résumé in about forty-five minutes, if Rich had had an existing résumé he could have updated and printed it in less than five minutes (and avoided all that stress). Preparing even a basic résumé from "scratch" takes time and invariably you need one just when you already have lots of other things to do.

Revisions are easy. If there are no additions or corrections, change only the file name (see Chapter 4 for specific instructions) and the date at the bottom of the first page in your file. Even adding major accomplishments usually takes less than fifteen minutes if you do it frequently.

> **Suggestion:** If you update your résumé twice without adding something, ask yourself if you are progressing the way you want. If the answer is yes, that's great. If not, complete the Personal Marketing Inventory to get some new ideas for skills you could hone or acquire.

Label a computer disk "Résumé and Personal Statement" and back it up. Dedicate one disk to your résumé and personal statement, and don't put other files on it. Label the disk with your name, address, college, and telephone number just in case you lose it or leave it in a wayward computer. Store the disk in a sturdy container to protect it. Since no computer disk lasts forever, make a "back-up" copy of your disk, label it, and keep it in a safe place. See Chapter 4 for complete directions. Be sure to also save your file in ASCII.

Concluding comments

Self-development is a lifelong, continuous process. It includes self-assessment, goal-setting, establishing priorities, selecting activities, assessing progress, and recording accomplishments. Academic, extracurricular, and personal activities help you develop as a health care professional throughout your career. Self-development takes time, energy, and effort, because it rarely happens by accident. Faculty, supervisors, administrators, and mentors can help you, but the final responsibility is yours. Visualize yourself in five and ten years. What will you be and what will you have accomplished? Do these visions match your goals? If not, what can you do to make your life goals happen? I hope this chapter inspires you to continue to seek new challenges throughout your life, and to participate in activities that will benefit you and help others.

GLOSSARY

Cover letter: A concise letter that states that you wish to apply for a position and gives information that is usually not found on one's résumé (e.g., why you want a position).

Curriculum Vitae: A synonym for résumé. It is usually used in academic circles. (abbreviated CV)

Foreign Medical Graduate (FMG): Any non-United States citizen who graduates from a foreign medical school.

Foreign Medical school: Any medical school not in the United States, Canada or Puerto Rico.

International Medical Graduate (IMG): Any American citizen who graduates from a foreign medical school, and any individual who graduates from a U.S., Canadian or accredited Puerto Rican medical school.

"Must/Want" Analysis: A process for selecting applicants used by selection committees and employers. A "Must" is a skill that is required for the position. A "Want" is a skill that employers desire, but they would not necessarily eliminate a person who lacks that quality. (See Chapter 8 in this text and K.V. Iserson's *Getting into a Residency: A Guide for Medical Students.*)

Personal Experience Inventory: A tool that helps you recall and organize information to put in your résumé.

Personal Marketing Inventory: A tool that helps you *analyze* academic, extracurricular, and personal experiences, and *specify* marketable attributes to put in your personal statement.

Personal Statement: A document, usually one page in length, that tells potential employers *who* you are. Used to explain the experiences, attitudes, and goals that shaped your life.

Résumé: A document that summarizes your career accomplishments and qualifications. It tells readers what you have done and it suggests your future potential.

Thank-you letter: A concise letter that expresses your appreciation for the courtesies extended to you during an interview, states interesting aspects of interviews with specific people, and describes your continued interest in the position.

BIBLIOGRAPHY

Academic Physician and Scientist. A bimonthly journal collaboratively published by Academic Physician Services and the Association of American Medical Colleges. (907 Embarcadero, Suite 4, El Dorado Hills, CA 95762; 916-939-4242; also available on Internet: Gopher.acad_phy_sci.com) This free journal contains relevant articles about medical education. It also lists information about basic science, clinical science, and administrative positions in academic medicine.

National Business Employment Weekly. Dow Jones & Company, Inc., P.O. Box 300, Princeton, NJ 08543. This weekly newsletter lists business-related job advertisements. It is also a great source of information about résumés, interviews, relocation guidance, and other related topics. A single copy costs about $4.00.

The Electronic Residency Application Service: Feasibility Report of the ERAS Advisory Committee. Association of American Medical Colleges, Washington, D.C., February 1994.

FRIEDA (Fellowship and Residency Electronic Interactive Database Access System). American Medical Association, 515 N. State St., Chicago, IL 60610. FRIEDA is a computerized system, updated yearly, that contains specific information about medical residencies and fellowships. You can use the program to prepare a database from which to write letters and print mailing labels. Institutions pay about $500 for one FRIEDA software package. Your local medical library or the computer laboratory at a medical school will probably have FRIEDA.

Graduate Medical Education Directory (the "Green Book"). American Medical Association, 515 N. State St., Chicago, IL 60610. The "Green Book" (yes, it *is* green) is published yearly and contains information about specialty and subspecialty graduate medical education training programs that are accredited by the Accreditation Council for Graduate Medical Education (ACGME). It gives contact information for all accredited programs within a specialty or subspecialty in each state. Usually in the reference section of your local medical library.

What Color is Your Parachute? A Practical Manual for Job-Hunters & Career-Changers. 1994. By Richard N. Bolles, Ten Speed Press, Berkeley, CA. This general reference is "must" reading for anyone who is considering changing jobs. The book provides strategies for getting and succeeding in interviews and offers tactics to assess your job skills. Check your local bookstore or library.

Getting into a Residency: A Guide for Medical Students, 3rd Ed. 1993. By Kenneth V. Iserson, M.D., Galen Press, Tucson, AZ. "Must" reading for pre-med, osteopathic, and medical students as they plan and move toward residency training. It gives specifics on the medical specialties and how to select one that's right for you. Equally important, it tells you how to navigate through the residency "match" process by providing suggestions on how to select a mentor, prepare application materials, and perform well during interviews. This book may also interest other health-professions students as the information on choosing the right program can be easily adapted to their needs. You can obtain the book in your medical library or bookstore, or you can order it from the publisher.

Index

This is not my copy and I need one for myself.

Résumés and Personal Statements for Health Professionals

by James W. Tysinger, Ph.D.

I also need a copy of:

GETTING INTO A RESIDENCY
A Guide for Medical Students

Third edition -- revised and enlarged
by Kenneth V. Iserson, M.D.

Order Form

Yes! . . . Please send me

Résumés and Personal Statements
for Health Professionals

Payment is enclosed (U.S. Funds Only)

[ ] Check   [ ] Money Order   [ ] Credit Card

Send me _____ copies @ $15.95 each $_____
    7% Sales Tax (AZ RESIDENTS ONLY: $1.12/BOOK) $_____
Send me _____ copies of *Getting Into A Residency*
    @ $ 28.95 each $_____
    7% Sales Tax (AZ RESIDENTS ONLY: $2.03/BOOK) $_____
Ship/Handling: $3.00 for 1st Book, $1.00/each additional $_____
Priority Mail: **Add** $2.95/book $_____

           TOTAL ENCLOSED $_____

SHIP TO:
Name: _____
Address: _____
_____
City/State/Zip _____

Send completed form and payment to:

Galen Press, Ltd.
PO Box 64400
Tucson, AZ 85728-4400

Tel (602)-577-8363
Fax (602)-529-6459

CREDIT CARD: ❏ **Visa**   ❏ **Mastercard**

Number: _____   Expiration date: _____

Signature: _____   Phone: (____) _____